Modern Library Chronicles

The American Revolution

GORDON S. WOOD

THE AMERICAN
REVOLUTION

A History

A MODERN LIBRARY CHRONICLES BOOK

THE MODERN LIBRARY

NEW YORK

LIBRARY OF CONGRESS CATALOGING-IN-PUBLICATION DATA
Wood, Gordon S.
The American revolution : a history / Gordon S. Wood.—
Modern library ed.
p.   cm.
ISBN 0-8129-7041-1
1. United States—History—Revolution, 1775–1783.   2. United
States—History—Revolution, 1775–1783—Causes.   I. Title.
E208 .W85 2001
973.3—dc21
2001044386

Modern Library website address: www.modernlibrary.com

Printed in the United States of America

14 16 18 17 15

ACKNOWLEDGMENTS

My thanks to Scott Moyers of Random House and to my wife Louise and my daughter Amy for their expert editorial assistance. My thanks also to Houghton Mifflin for permission to use portions of my section of *The Great Republic* by Bernard Bailyn et al.

CONTENTS

MAPS

CHRONOLOGY

1768

February 11	Samuel Adams composes the Massachusetts "circular letter"
June 8	British troops are sent to Boston

1770

March 5	Boston Massacre
April 12	The Townshend duties are repealed, except for the duty on tea

1772

June 9	The British ship *Gaspée* burned off Rhode Island
November 2	Bostonians publish *The Votes and Proceedings*, enumerating British violations of American rights

1773

January 6	Massachusetts governor Hutchinson argues the supremacy of Parliament before the General Court
May 10	Parliament passes the Tea Act
December 16	Boston Tea Party

1774

March 31–June 22	Parliament passes the Coercive Acts and the Quebec Act
September 5–October 26	First Continental Congress meets in Philadelphia

1775

April 18	Paul Revere's ride
April 19	Battles of Lexington and Concord
May 10	American forces capture Fort Ticonderoga on Lake Champlain

May 10	Second Continental Congress convenes
June 15	George Washington is appointed commander of the Continental Army
June 17	Battle of Bunker Hill
August 23	King George III declares the colonies in open rebellion
December 31	Colonists are defeated at Quebec

1776

January 10	Thomas Paine publishes *Common Sense*
March 17	British troops evacuate Boston
July 4	Continental Congress approves the Declaration of Independence
August 27	Battle of Long Island, New York; British take New York City
December 25–26	Washington crosses the Delaware River; battle of Trenton

1777

January 3	Battle of Princeton
September 11	Battle of Brandywine
October 4	Washington is defeated at Germantown; his army retires to Valley Forge for winter
October 17	British general Burgoyne surrenders at Saratoga
November 15	Articles of Confederation are approved by Congress and sent to states for ratification

1778

February 6	France and the United States form an alliance

1780

May 12	British capture Charleston, South Carolina

| September 25 | Benedict Arnold flees to the British after spying for them for more than a year |
| October 7 | British general Cornwallis's troops are forced to retreat from North Carolina |

1781

January 17	Battle of Cowpens, South Carolina
March 1	Articles of Confederation are ratified
March 15	Battle of Guilford Courthouse, North Carolina
October 19	Cornwallis surrenders to Washington at Yorktown, Virginia

1783

| September 3 | Treaty of Peace between the Americans and British is signed |

1786

| August | Shays's Rebellion in western Massachusetts |
| September 11 | Annapolis Convention |

1787

May 25	Constitutional Convention opens in Philadelphia
July 13	Northwest Ordinance is enacted by Congress
September 17	Constitutional Convention approves the newly drafted Constitution and sends it to Congress
October 27	First of Hamilton, Madison, and Jay's *Federalist Papers* appears

1788

January–August   Ratification of U.S. Constitution by all states except Rhode Island and North Carolina

1789

March 4   First U.S. Congress under the Constitution convenes in New York

April 30   George Washington is inaugurated first president of the United States

· 1791

December 15   First ten amendments to Constitution (the Bill of Rights) are adopted

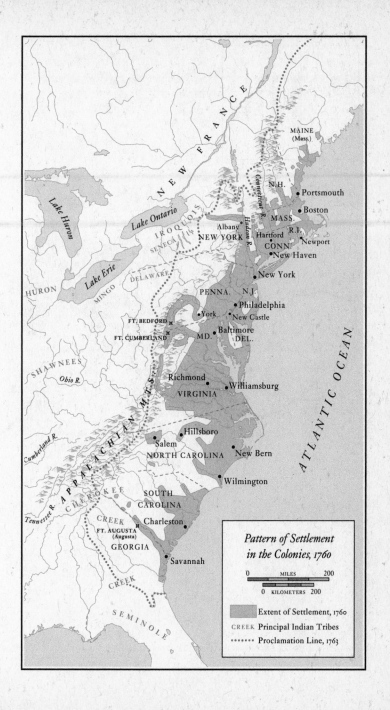

LAKE HURON

Lake Huron

Lake Erie

Lake Ontario

NEW FRANCE

IROQUOIS

SENECA

HURON

MINGO

DELAWARE

SHAWNEES

Ohio R.

APPALACHIAN MTS.

Cumberland R.

Tennessee R.

CHEROKEE

CREEK

FT. AUGUSTA
(Augusta)

CREEK

SEMINOLE

MAINE
(Mass.)

N.H.

Portsmouth

Boston

MASS.

Albany

Hartford

R.I.

NEW YORK

CONN.

Newport

New Haven

New York

PENNA.

N.J.

Philadelphia

York

New Castle

FT. BEDFORD

FT. CUMBERLAND

Baltimore

MD.

DEL.

Richmond

Williamsburg

VIRGINIA

Hillsboro

Salem

NORTH CAROLINA

New Bern

Wilmington

SOUTH
CAROLINA

Charleston

GEORGIA

Savannah

ATLANTIC OCEAN

Connecticut R.

Hudson R.

*Pattern of Settlement
in the Colonies, 1760*

0   MILES   200

0   KILOMETERS   200

Extent of Settlement, 1760

CREEK   Principal Indian Tribes

•••••• Proclamation Line, 1763

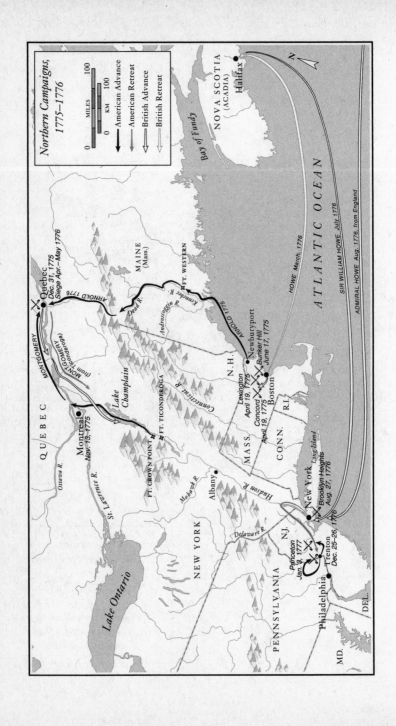

Northern Campaigns,
1775–1776

MILES
0   100

KM
0   100

→ American Advance
→ American Retreat
⇒ British Advance
⇒ British Retreat

ATLANTIC OCEAN

HOWE March 1776

SIR WILLIAM HOWE Aug. 1776 from England

ADMIRAL HOWE Aug. 1776, from England

NOVA SCOTIA
(ACADIA)

Halifax

Bay of Fundy

MAINE
(Mass.)

FT. WESTERN

Kennebec R.

Dead R.

ARNOLD 1775

Androscoggin R.

Quebec
Dec. 31, 1775
Siege Apr.–May 1776

ARNOLD 1776

MONTGOMERY
(from Ticonderoga)

MONTGOMERY

QUEBEC

Ottawa R.

St. Lawrence R.

Montreal
Nov. 13, 1775

Lake
Champlain

FT. TICONDEROGA

FT. CROWN POINT

Connecticut R.

N.H.

Newburyport

Bunker Hill
June 17, 1775

Lexington
April 19, 1775

Concord
April 19, 1775

Boston

MASS.

R.I.

CONN.

Mohawk R.

Albany

NEW YORK

Hudson R.

New York

Long Island

Brooklyn Heights
Aug. 27, 1776

Delaware R.

N.J.

Princeton
Jan. 3, 1777

Trenton
Dec. 25–26, 1776

Philadelphia

PENNSYLVANIA

MD.

DEL.

Lake Ontario

N

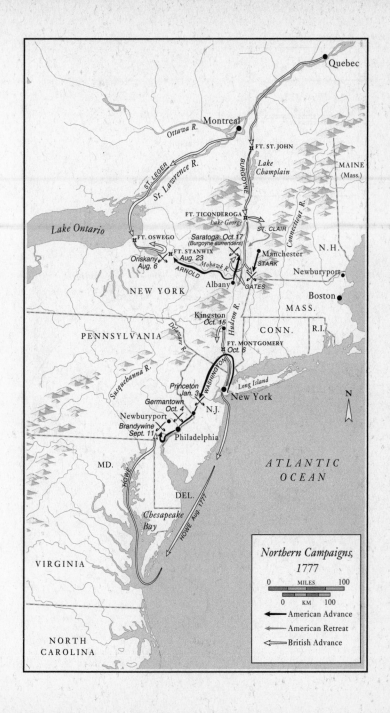

Quebec

Montreal

Ottawa R.

FT. ST. JOHN

St. LEGER

St. Lawrence R.

BURGOYNE

Lake Champlain

MAINE (Mass.)

Connecticut R.

Lake Ontario

FT. TICONDEROGA
Lake George

FT. OSWEGO

ST. CLAIR

N.H.

Saratoga Oct. 17
(Burgoyne surrenders)

FT. STANWIX
Aug. 23

Manchester

Oriskany
Aug. 6

STARK

ARNOLD

Mohawk R.

Newburyport

NEW YORK

Albany

GATES

Boston

MASS.

Kingston
Oct. 15

Hudson R.

CONN.

R.I.

PENNSYLVANIA

Delaware R.

FT. MONTGOMERY
Oct. 6

WASHINGTON

Susquehanna R.

Princeton
Jan. 3

Long Island

Germantown
Oct. 4

N.J.

New York

Newburyport

Brandywine
Sept. 11

Philadelphia

N

MD.

HOWE

ATLANTIC
OCEAN

DEL.

HOWE Aug. 1777

Chesapeake
Bay

VIRGINIA

*Northern Campaigns,
1777*

0   MILES   100

0   KM   100

⬅ American Advance

← American Retreat

⇐ British Advance

NORTH
CAROLINA

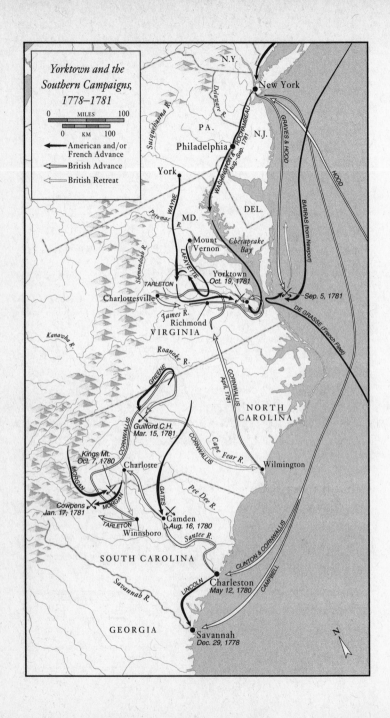

Yorktown and the
Southern Campaigns,
1778–1781

0   MILES   100

0   KM   100

→ American and/or
   French Advance
⇐ British Advance
⇐ British Retreat

PREFACE

When in the midst of the Civil War Abraham Lincoln sought to define the significance of the United States, he naturally looked back to the American Revolution. He knew that the Revolution not only had legally created the United States, but also had produced all of the great hopes and values of the American people. The noblest ideals and aspirations of Americans—their commitments to freedom, constitutionalism, the well-being of ordinary people, and equality, especially equality—came out of the Revolutionary era. But Lincoln saw as well that the Revolution had convinced Americans that they were a special people with a special destiny to lead the world toward liberty. The Revolution, in short, gave birth to whatever sense of nationhood and national purpose Americans have had.

Such a momentous event has inevitably attracted successive generations of historical interpretation. At the outset Americans saw their Revolution as a heroic moral struggle for liberty against the evils of British tyranny, with the participants being larger-than-life heroes or villains. Then through much of the nineteenth century, largely through the work of George Bancroft, the Revolution lost some of its highly personal character and became the providential fulfillment of the American people's democratic destiny, something preordained from the very beginning of the seventeenth-century colonial settlements. And like the nation it produced, it was exceptional. Unlike the French Revolution, which had been caused by actual tyranny, the American Revolution was seen as a peculiarly intellectual and conservative affair, as something brought about not by actual oppression but by the anticipation of oppression, by reasoning and devotion to principle, such as "no taxation without representation."

Only at the beginning of the twentieth century and the birth of professional history-writing did the Revolution become something more than a colonial rebellion and something other than a conservative intellectual event. As Carl Becker, one of the leading historians at the time, put it, the Revolution was not only about home rule; it was also about who should rule at home. And it was now seen as anything but a contest over ideas. This denigration of ideas and emphasis on class and sectional conflict dominated history-writing during the first half of the twentieth century. Then at mid-century a new generation of historians rediscovered the constitutional and conservative character of the Revolution and carried the intellectual interpretation of the Revolution to new heights of sophistication.

Although American historians had disagreed with one another over these two centuries of changing interpretations, they had rarely if ever questioned the worth of the Revolution. At present, however, the Revolution, like the nation it created, has come in for some very serious criticism. Indeed, it has become fashionable to deny that anything substantially progressive came out of the Revolution. Instead, some historians today are more apt to stress the failures of the Revolution. As one young historian recently put it, the Revolution "failed to free the slaves, failed to offer full political equality to women,…failed to grant citizenship to Indians, [and] failed to create an economic world in which all could compete on equal terms." Such anachronistic statements suggest a threshold of success that no eighteenth-century revolution could possibly have attained, and perhaps tell us more about the political attitudes of the historians who make such statements than they do about the American Revolution. In some sense these present-day critical historians have simply inverted the first generation's heroic celebration of the Revolution.

The history of the American Revolution, like the history of the nation as a whole, ought not to be viewed as a story of right and wrong or good and evil from which moral lessons are to be drawn. No doubt the story of the Revolution is a dramatic one: Thirteen insignificant British colonies huddled along a narrow strip of the Atlantic coast three thousand miles from the centers of Western civilization becoming in fewer than three decades a huge, sprawling republic of nearly 4 million expansive-minded, evangelical, and money-hungry citizens is a spectacular tale, to say the least. But the Revolution, like the whole of American history, is not a simple morality play; it is a complicated and often ironic story that needs to be explained and understood, not celebrated or condemned. How the Revolution came about, what its character was, and what its consequences were—not whether it was good or bad—are the questions this brief history seeks to answer.

I

ORIGINS

The origins of the Revolution necessarily lie deep in America's past. A century and a half of dynamic developments in the British continental colonies of the New World had fundamentally transformed inherited European institutions and customary patterns of life and had left many colonists believing that they were seriously deviating from the cultivated norms of European life. In comparison with prosperous and powerful metropolitan England, America in the middle of the eighteenth century seemed a primitive, backward place, disordered and turbulent, without a real aristocracy, without magnificent courts or large urban centers, indeed, without any of the attributes of the civilized world. Consequently, the colonists repeatedly felt pressed to apologize for the crudity of their society, the insignificance of their art and literature, and the triviality of their affairs.

Suddenly in the 1760s Great Britain thrust its imperial power into this changing world with a thoroughness that had not been felt in a century and precipitated a crisis within the loosely organized empire. American resistance turned into rebellion; but as the colonists groped to make sense of the peculiarities of their society, this rebellion became a justification and idealization of American life as it had gradually and unintentionally developed over the previous century and a half. Instead of being in the backwaters of history, Americans suddenly saw themselves as a new society ideally equipped for a republican future. In this sense, as John Adams later said, "the Revolution was effected before the war commenced." It was a change "in the minds and hearts of the people."

But this change was not the whole American Revolution. The Revolution was not simply an intellectual endorsement of a previously existing social reality. It was also an integral part of the great transforming process that carried America into the liberal democratic society of the modern world. Although colonial America was already a different place from Europe in 1760, it still retained, along with powdered wigs and knee breeches, many traditional habits of monarchical behavior and dependent social relationships. The Revolution shattered what remained of these traditional patterns of life and prepared the way for the more fluid, bustling, individualistic world that followed.

The changes were remarkable, and they gave the American people as grand a vision of their future as any people have ever had. Americans saw their new nation not only leading a world revolution on behalf of republicanism and liberty but also becoming the place where the best of all the arts and sciences would flourish. What began as a colonial rebellion on the very edges of the civilized world was transformed into an earth-shaking event—an event that promised, as one clergyman declared, to create out of the "perishing World ... a new World, a young world, a World of countless Millions, all in the fair Bloom of Piety."

THE GROWTH AND MOVEMENT OF POPULATION

In 1763, Great Britain straddled the world with the greatest and richest empire since the fall of Rome. From India to the Mississippi River its armies and navies had been victorious. The Peace of Paris that concluded the Seven Years' War— or the French and Indian War, as the Americans called it— gave Britain undisputed dominance over the eastern half of North America. From the defeated powers, France and Spain, Britain acquired huge chunks of territory in the New World—all of Canada, East and West Florida, and millions of fertile acres between the Appalachian Mountains and the Mississippi River. France turned over to Spain the territory of

Louisiana in compensation for Spain's loss of Florida; and thus this most fearsome of Britain's enemies removed itself altogether from the North American continent.

Yet at the moment of Britain's supremacy there were powerful forces at work that would soon, almost overnight, change everything. In the aftermath of the Seven Years' War, British officials found themselves having to make long-postponed decisions concerning the colonies that would set in motion a chain of events that ultimately shattered the empire.

Ever since the formation of the British Empire in the late seventeenth century, royal officials and bureaucrats had been interested in reforming the ramshackle imperial structure and in expanding royal authority over the American colonists. But most of their schemes had been blocked by English ministries more concerned with the patronage of English politics than with colonial reform. Under such circumstances the empire had been allowed to grow haphazardly, without much control from London. People from different places in Europe had been allowed to settle in the colonies, and land had been given out freely.

Although few imperial officials had ever doubted that the colonies were supposed to be inferior to the mother country and dependent on it, in fact the empire had not worked that way. The relationship that had developed reflected the irrational and inefficient nature of the imperial system—the variety of offices, the diffusion of power, and the looseness of organization. Even in trade regulation, which was the empire's main business, inefficiency, loopholes, and numerous opportunities for corruption prevented the imperial authorities from interfering substantively with the colonists' pursuit of their own economic and social interests.

By the middle of the eighteenth century, however, new circumstances began forcing changes in this irrational but working relationship. The British colonies—there were twenty-two of them in the Western Hemisphere in 1760—were becoming too important to be treated as casually as the mother country had treated them in the first half of the eighteenth century. Dynamic developments throughout the greater British world demanded that England pay more attention to its North American colonies.

The most basic of these developments were the growth and movement of population. In the middle decades of the eighteenth century, the number of people throughout the whole English-speaking world—in Britain and the colonies alike—was increasing at unprecedented rates. During the 1740s the population of England, which had hardly grown at all for half a century, suddenly began to increase. The populations of Ireland and Scotland had been rising steadily since the beginning of the eighteenth century. The population of the North American colonies was growing even faster— virtually exploding—and had been doing so almost since the beginning of the settlements. Indeed, the North American colonists continued to multiply more rapidly than any other people in the Western world. Between 1750 and 1770 they doubled in number, from 1 million to more than 2 million, and thereby became an even more important part of the British world. In 1700 the American population had been only one twentieth of the British and Irish populations combined; by 1770 it was nearly one fifth, and such farsighted colonists as Benjamin Franklin were predicting that sooner or later the center of the British Empire would shift to America.

Everywhere the expanding British population was in motion, moving from village to village and from continent to continent. In Britain growing numbers of migrants in a few decades created the new industrial cities of Birmingham, Manchester, and Leeds and made London the largest urban center in the Western world. A steady stream moved from the British Isles across the Atlantic to the New World. The migration of Protestant Irish and Scots that had begun early in the century increased after the Seven Years' War of the 1750s. Between 1764 and 1776 some 125,000 people left the British

Isles for the American colonies. From the colonial port towns, particularly Philadelphia, British immigrants and Germans from the Rhine Valley joined with increasing numbers of colonists to spread over half a continent along a variety of routes.

For nearly a century and a half the colonists had been confined to a several-hundred-mile-wide strip of territory along the Atlantic coast. But in the middle decades of the eighteenth century, the pressures of increasing population density began to be felt. Overcultivated soil in the East was becoming depleted. Particularly in the Chesapeake areas the number of tenants was visibly growing. Older towns now seemed overcrowded, especially in New England, and young men coming of age could no longer count on obtaining pieces of land as their fathers had done. Throughout the colonies more and more people were on the move; many drifted into the small colonial cities, which were ill equipped to handle them. By 1772 in Philadelphia, the percentage of poor was eight times greater than it had been twenty years earlier, and almshouses were being constructed and filled as never before. Most of these transient poor, however, saw the cities only as way stations in their endless search for land on which they might re-create the stability they had been forced to abandon.

With the defeat of the French, people set out in all directions, eager to take advantage of the newly acquired land in the interior. In 1759 speculators and settlers moved into the area around Lake Champlain and westward along the Mohawk River into central New York. Between 1749 and 1771, New York's population grew from 73,348 to 168,007. Tens of thousands of colonists and new immigrants pushed into western Pennsylvania and southward into the Carolinas along routes on each side of Virginia's Blue Ridge. Along these roads strings of towns—from York, Pennsylvania, to Camden, South Carolina—quickly developed to service the travelers and to distribute produce to distant markets. The growth of settlement was phenomenal. In Pennsylvania twenty-nine new localities were created between 1756 and 1765—more in these few years than in the colony's entire previous history. North Carolina increased its population sixfold between 1750 and 1775 to become the fourth-largest colony.

New frontiers appeared everywhere throughout British North America. By the early 1760s hunters and explorers such as Daniel Boone began opening up paths westward through the Appalachians. Settlers soon followed. Some moved southward to the valley of the Holston River and to the headwaters of the Cumberland and Tennessee Rivers, and others spread northwest into the Ohio Valley and the Kentucky basin. Some drifted down the Ohio and Mississippi Rivers to join overland migrants from the southern colonies in the new province of West Florida, and thus completed a huge encirclement of the new western territory.

During the decade and a half before Independence, New England throbbed with movement. By the early 1760s the number of transients drifting from town to town throughout the region multiplied dramatically, in some counties doubling or tripling the numbers of the previous decade. Many farmers gave up searching for opportunities within established communities and set out for distant places on the very edges of the expanded empire. Massachusetts and Connecticut colonists trekked not only to northern New England and Nova Scotia, but to areas as far away as the Susquehanna River in Pennsylvania and the lower Mississippi River. Indeed, the largest single addition to the population of West Florida came from the settlement of four hundred families from Connecticut in 1773–74. Between 1760 and 1776 some 20,000 people from southern New England moved up the Connecticut River into New Hampshire and into what would later become Vermont. In that same period migrants from Massachusetts streamed into Maine and founded 94 towns. A total of 264 new towns were established in northern New England during the years between 1760 and 1776.

British and colonial authorities could scarcely comprehend the meaning of this enormous explosion of people in search of land. The colonists, one astonished official observed, were moving "as their avidity and restlessness incite them. They acquire no attachment to place: but wandering about seems engrafted in their nature; and it is a weakness incident to it that they should forever imagine the lands further off are still better than those upon which they are already settled." Land fever infected all levels of society. While Ezra Stiles, a minister in Newport, Rhode Island, and later the president of Yale University, bought and sold small shares in places all over New England and in Pennsylvania and New York, more influential figures like Benjamin Franklin were concocting huge speculative schemes in the vast unsettled lands of the West.

All this movement had far-reaching effects on American society and its place in the British Empire. The fragmentation of households, churches, and communities increased, and the colonial governments lost control of the mushrooming new settlements. In the backcountry, lawlessness and vagrancy became common, and disputes over land claims and colonial boundaries increased sharply. But the most immediate effect of this rapid spread of people—and the effect that was most obvious to imperial officials by mid-century—was the pressure that the migrations placed on the native peoples.

At the beginning of the Seven Years' War, the problems of restless and angry Native Americans in the West compelled the British government for the first time to take over from the colonies the direct control of Indian affairs. Two British officials, one each for the northern and southern regions, now had the task of pacifying tribes of Indians, whom one of the superintendents described as "the most formidable of any uncivilized body of people in the world."

Although the European invasion of the New World had drastically reduced the numbers of the native peoples, largely through the spread of disease, about 150,000 Indians remained in the area east of the Mississippi. New England had

few hostile Indians, but in New York there were 2,000 warriors, mostly fierce Senecas, left from the once formidable Six
Nations of the Iroquois. In the Susquehanna and Ohio Val-
leys dwelled a variety of tribes, mostly Delawares, Shawnees,
Mingos, and Hurons, who claimed about 12,000 fighting men.
On the southern frontiers the Indian presence was even more
forbidding. From the Carolinas to the Yazoo River were some
14,000 warriors, mainly Cherokees, Creeks, Chocktaws, and
Chickasaws. Although these native peoples were often deeply
divided from one another and had reached different degrees
of accommodation with the European settlers, most of them
were anxious to resist further white encroachment on their
lands.

After French authority had been eliminated from Canada
and Spanish authority from Florida, the Native Americans
were no longer able to play one European power off against
the other. Britain now had sole responsibility for regulating
the profitable fur trade and for maintaining peace between
whites and Indians. The problems were awesome. Not only
were many whites prepared to use brandy and rum to achieve
their aims, but they had conflicting interests. Some traders favored regulation of the fur trade, and others did not. But all
traders favored the establishment in the West of Indian reser-
vations that settlers would not be permitted to invade, and
they drew on the support of humanitarian groups who were
concerned with the Indians' fate. Land speculators, however,
wanted to move the Indians westward and open more territory for white settlement. Confused, lied to, and cheated of
their land and their furs by greedy white traders and land-
hungry migrants, the Indians retaliated with atrocities and
raids. Some tribes attempted to form coalitions and wage full-
scale war.

Thus the end of the Seven Years' War did not end violence on the frontier. From the devastating Cherokee War of
1759–61 in South Carolina to the assault on the Shawnees in

1774 by Lord Dunmore, the royal governor of Virginia, British officials repeatedly had to use royal troops to put down Indian revolts. The biggest Indian rebellion of the period occurred in 1763 following the British takeover of the former French forts in the West. In just a few weeks Indians from several tribes that had joined together under the leadership of an Ottawa chief named Pontiac surprised and destroyed all but three of the British posts west of the Appalachians. Before they were pushed back by British troops, the angry warriors had penetrated eastward into the backcountry of Pennsylvania, Maryland, and Virginia and had killed more than 2,000 colonists. It is no wonder that many royal authorities in the 1760s concluded that only the presence of regular troops of the British army could maintain peace in the American borderlands of the empire.

The rapid growth and spread of people in the mid eighteenth century affected more than white-Indian relations on the frontier. Thousands of migrants flowed into the backcountry, beyond the reach of the eastern colonial governments. These backcountry settlers were so distant from legal authority that sometimes vigilante groups had to impose order. In the 1760s backcountry people in South Carolina organized vigilante "Regulators" to put down roving gangs of thieves, but extralegal posses of this kind often turned into raiders themselves. Sometimes frontiersmen in these trans-Appalachian areas of the West came together to form compacts of government for their raw societies, which often consisted of little more than "stations"—primitive stockaded forts surrounded by huts.

Everywhere in the backcountry the sudden influx of people weakened the legitimacy of existing authority. In the rapidly growing interiors of Pennsylvania and North Carolina, settlers in the 1760s rose in arms against what they believed was exploitation by remote eastern governments. In western Pennsylvania, Scotch-Irish settlers led by the Paxton

Boys rebelled against the Quaker-dominated, pacifist-minded Pennsylvania assembly, in which they were grossly under-represented. In 1763–64 they killed Indians who were under the government's protection and then marched on Philadelphia. The rebels turned back only after mediation by Benjamin Franklin and the promise of a greater voice in the eastern-controlled colonial assembly. In North Carolina not only was the backcountry underrepresented in the provincial legislature, but the local county courts were under the corrupt management of carpetbagging officials and lawyers from the eastern part of the colony. In 1767 a group of western vigilantes, assuming the familiar title Regulators, erupted in violence. They took over the county courts and petitioned the North Carolina government for greater representation, lower taxes, and local control of their affairs. Two thousand of these Regulators were dispersed by the North Carolina governor and his force of eastern militia at the so-called battle of Alamance in 1771. But royal officials could not so easily dispel the deeply rooted fears among many Americans of the dangers of unfair representation and distant political power. Indeed these westerners were only voicing toward their own colonial governments the same attitudes that Americans in general had about British power.

ECONOMIC EXPANSION

All these consequences flowing from the increased numbers of people in North America were bound to raise Britain's interest in its colonies. But population pressures were not all that were reshaping British attitudes toward the colonies and transforming American society. Equally important was the remarkable expansion of the Anglo-American economy taking place in the middle years of the eighteenth century.

By 1750 in Britain the immediate origins of what would soon become the industrial revolution were already visible.

British imports, exports, and industrial production of various sorts—all the major indicators of economic growth—were rapidly rising. Americans were deeply involved in this sudden British economic expansion, and by 1760 they were prospering as never before.

In the years after 1745, colonial trade with Great Britain grew dramatically and became an increasingly important segment of the English and Scottish economies. Nearly half of all English shipping was engaged in American commerce. The North American mainland was absorbing 25 percent of English exports, and Scottish commercial involvement with the colonies was growing even more rapidly. From 1747 to 1765 the value of colonial exports to Britain doubled from about £700,000 to £1.5 million, while the value of colonial imports from Britain rose even faster, from about £900,000 to more than £2 million. For the first time in the eighteenth century, Britain's own production of foodstuffs could not meet the needs of its suddenly rising population. By 1760, Britain was importing more grain than it exported. This increasing demand for foodstuffs—not only in Great Britain, but in southern Europe and the West Indies as well—meant soaring prices for American exports. Between the 1740s and the 1760s, the price of American produce exported to the Caribbean increased by huge percentages. Seeing the greater demand and rising prices for American exports, more and more ordinary farmers began to produce foodstuffs and other goods for distant markets. By the 1760s remote trading centers in the backcountry such as Staunton, Virginia, and Salisbury, North Carolina, were shipping large quantities of tobacco and grain eastward to the sea along networks of roads and towns. Port cities like Baltimore, Norfolk, and Alexandria grew up almost overnight to handle this swelling traffic.

Soaring prices for agricultural exports meant rising standards of living for more and more Americans. It was not just the great planters of the South and the big merchants of the cities who were getting richer. Now ordinary Americans were also buying luxury items that traditionally had been purchased only by wealthy gentry—items that were increasingly called conveniences and that ranged from Irish linen and lace to matched sets of Wedgwood dishes. Benjamin Franklin tells us in his autobiography that his wife Deborah surprised him one morning with some new replacements for his pewter spoon and earthen bowl. By purchasing these items simply because "she thought her Husband deserved a Silver Spoon & China Bowl as well as any of his Neighbours," she was raising her family's status and standard of living. At the same time, she was contributing to what historians have come to call an eighteenth-century "consumer revolution."

Although nineteen out of twenty Americans were still engaged in agriculture, the rising levels of taste and consumption drew more colonists into manufacturing—at first, mostly the production of crude textiles and shoes. Transportation and communications rapidly improved as roads were built and regular schedules were established for stagecoaches and packet boats. In the 1750s the Post Office, under the leadership of Benjamin Franklin, the colonial deputy postmaster general, instituted weekly mails between Philadelphia and Boston and cut delivery time in half, from six to three weeks. The growing population, better roads, more reliable information about markets, and the greater variety of towns all encouraged domestic manufacturing for regional and intercolonial markets. By 1768 colonial manufacturers were supplying Pennsylvania with eight thousand pairs of shoes a year. Areas of eastern Massachusetts were becoming more involved in manufacturing: in 1767 the town of Haverhill, with fewer than three hundred residents, had forty-four workshops and nineteen mills. By this date many colonial artisans and would-be manufacturers were more than eager to support associations to boycott rival English imports.

But most colonists still preferred British goods. From the late 1740s on, Americans were importing from Britain about

£500,000 worth of goods more than they were exporting to the mother country, and thus they continued to be troubled by a trade deficit with Britain. Part of this deficit in the colonists' balance of payments with Britain was made up by the profits of shipping, by British wartime expenditures in America, and by increased sales to Europe and the West Indies. But a large part was also made up by the extension to the colonists of large amounts of English and Scottish credit. By 1760 colonial debts to Britain amounted to £2 million; by 1772 they had jumped to more than £4 million. After 1750 a growing proportion of this debt was owed by colonists who earlier had been excluded from direct dealings with British merchants. More and more small tobacco farmers in the Chesapeake gained immediate access to British credit and markets through the spread of Scottish "factors" (storekeepers) in the backcountry of Virginia and Maryland. By 1760 it was not unusual for as many as 150 petty traders in a single port to be doing business with a London merchant company.

These demographic and economic forces undermined the customary paternalistic structure of colonial society. The ties of kinship and patronage that traditionally held people together, which had never been strong in America to begin with, were now further weakened. Even in Virginia, one of the most stable of the colonies, the leading aristocratic plantation owners found their authority challenged by small farmers who were no longer as personally dependent on them for credit and markets. These small farmers now forged more impersonal connections with the new Scottish factors and became more much independent than they had been before. They expressed this independence by becoming more involved in politics and by promoting religious dissent. During the middle decades of the eighteenth century, not only did the number of contested elections to the Virginia House of Burgesses increase markedly, but also ordinary people in Virginia began leaving the established Church of England in growing numbers. They formed new evangelical religious communities that rejected the high style and luxury of the dominant Anglican gentry. Within a few years succeeding waves of New Light Presbyterians, Separate Baptists, and finally Methodists swept up new converts from among the common farmers of the Chesapeake region. Between 1769 and 1774 the number of Baptist churches in Virginia increased from seven to fifty-four.

The Virginia gentry blamed the growth of religious dissent on the long-claimed incompetence of the Anglican ministers. In turn the ministers accused the lay vestries, which were composed of Anglican gentry, of not supporting them. Amid these mutual accusations the Virginia House of Burgesses passed acts in 1755 and 1758 that fixed at twopence a pound the standard value of tobacco used to meet debts and public obligations. Since tobacco prices were rising rapidly, these so-called Two-Penny Acts penalized creditors and those public officials (including ministers) who were used to being paid in tobacco. British merchants and the ministers of Virginia's established Anglican Church protested and were able to get the king's Privy Council in England to disallow the Burgesses' 1758 act. In 1763 a rising young lawyer, Patrick Henry, first made his reputation as a powerful popular orator in a court battle over one of the Virginia ministers' legal suits for the recovery of wages lost by the now illegal Two-Penny Act. In his defense of the Virginia planters against this "Parson's Cause," Henry went so far as to claim that, because the king had vetoed the act, he "from being the father of his people [has] degenerated into a Tyrant, and forfeits all rights to his subjects' obedience." That Henry could be celebrated for such histrionic (and seditious) remarks was a measure of how tenuous and brittle traditional relationships had become. Everywhere in the colonies, nerves were on edge and men were quick to blame all authority, including that of the king three thousand miles away, for the rapidly changing circumstances of their lives.

It is doubtful whether anyone anywhere in the mid eighteenth century knew how to control the powerful social and economic forces at work in the Anglo-American world. Certainly the flimsy administrative arrangement that governed the British Empire seemed scarcely capable of managing this incredibly dynamic world. No doubt by mid-century many British officials had come to realize that some sort of overhaul of this increasingly important empire was needed. But few understood the explosive energy and the sensitive nature of the people they were tampering with. The British Empire, Benjamin Franklin warned, was like a fragile Chinese vase that required delicate handling indeed.

REFORM OF THE BRITISH EMPIRE

After 1748 various imperial reforms were in the air. The eye-opening experience of fighting the Seven Years' War amid the colonists' evasion and corruption of the navigation laws had provoked William Pitt and other royal officials into vigorous, though piecemeal, reforms of the imperial system. But these beginnings might have been suppressed, as others earlier had been, if it had not been for the enormous problems that were created by the Peace of Paris, which ended the Seven Years' War in 1763.

The most immediate of these problems was the reorganization of the territory that had been acquired from France and Spain. New governments had to be organized, the Indian trade had to be regulated, land claims had to be sorted out, and something had to be done to keep the conflicts between land-hungry white settlers and angry Native Americans from exploding into open warfare.

Even more disturbing was the huge expense confronting the British government. By 1763 the war debt totaled £137 million; its annual interest alone was £5 million, a huge figure when compared with an ordinary yearly British peacetime budget of only £8 million. There was, moreover, little prospect of military costs declining. Since the new territories were virtually uninhabited by Englishmen, the government could not rely on its traditional system of local defense and police to preserve order. Lord Jeffrey Amherst, commander in chief in North America, estimated that he would need 10,000 troops to keep the peace with the French and Indians and to deal with squatters, smugglers, and bandits. Thus at the outset of the 1760s the British government made a crucial decision that no subsequent administration ever abandoned— the decision to maintain a standing army in America. This peacetime army was more than double the size of the army that had existed in the colonies before the Seven Years' War, and the costs of maintaining it quickly climbed to well over £300,000 a year.

Where was the money to come from? The landowning gentry in England felt pressed to the wall by taxes; a new English cider tax of 1763 actually required troops in the apple-growing counties of England to enforce it. Meanwhile, returning British troops were bringing home tales of the prosperity Americans were enjoying at the war's end. Under the circumstances it seemed reasonable to the British government to seek new sources of revenue in the colonies and to make the navigation system more efficient in ways that royal officials had long advocated. A half century of what Edmund Burke called "salutary neglect" had come to an end.

The delicate balance of this rickety empire was therefore bound to be disrupted. But the coming to the throne in 1760 of a new monarch, the young and impetuous George III, worsened this changing Anglo-American relationship. George III was only twenty-two years old at the time, shy and inexperienced in politics. But he was stubbornly determined to rule personally, in a manner distinctly different from that of the Hanoverians George I and George II, his German-born great-grandfather and grandfather. With the disastrous failure of the Stuart heir, "Bonnie Prince Charlie," to reclaim the English throne in 1745–46, George, who was the first of

the Hanoverian kings to be British-born, was much more confident of his hold on the throne than his Hanoverian prede-
cessors had been. Hence he felt freer to ignore the advice of
the Whig ministers, who had guided the first two Georges,
and to become his own ruler. Influenced by his inept Scottish
tutor and "dearest friend," Lord Bute, he aimed to purify English public life of its corruption and factionalism. He wanted
to replace former Whig-Tory squabbling and party intrigue
with duty to crown and country. These were the best of intentions, but the results of them were the greatest and most
bewildering fluctuations in English politics in a half century—
all at the very moment the long-postponed reforms of the
empire were to take place.

Historians no longer depict George III as a tyrant seeking to undermine the English constitution by choosing his
ministers against Parliament's wishes. But there can be little
doubt that men of the time felt that George III, whether he
meant to or not, was violating the political conventions of
the day. When he chose Lord Bute, his Scottish favorite, who
had little strength in Parliament, to head his government,
thereby excluding such Whig ministers as William Pitt and
the Duke of Newcastle, who did have political support in Parliament, the new king may not have been acting unconstitu-
tionally, but he certainly was violating customary political
realities. Bute's retirement in 1763 did little to ease the opposition's fears that the king was seeking the advice of Tory fa-
vorites "behind the curtain" and was attempting to impose
decisions on the leading political groups in Parliament rather
than governing through them. By diligently attempting to
shoulder what he thought was his constitutional responsibility
for governing in his own stubborn, peculiar way, George III
helped to increase the political confusion of the 1760s.

A decade of short-lived ministries in the 1760s contrasted
sharply with the stable and long-lasting Whig governments of
the previous generation. It almost seemed as if the stubborn
king trusted no one who had Parliament's support. After Pitt

and Newcastle had been dismissed, and after Bute had faded, the king in 1763 turned to George Grenville, Bute's protégé, only because he found no one else acceptable to be his chief minister. Although Grenville was responsible for the first wave of colonial reforms, his resignation in 1765 resulted from a personal quarrel with the king and had nothing to do with colonial policy. Next, a government was formed by Whigs who were connected with the Marquess of Rockingham and for whom the great orator and political thinker Edmund Burke was a spokesman; but this Whig coalition never had the king's confidence, and it lasted scarcely a year. In 1766, George at last called on the aging Pitt, now Lord Chatham, to head the government. But Chatham's illness (gout in the head, critics said) and the bewildering parliamentary factionalism of the late 1760s turned his ministry into such a hodgepodge that Chatham scarcely ruled at all.

By 1767 no one seemed to be in charge. Ministers shuffled in and out of offices, exchanging positions and following their own inclinations even against their colleagues' wishes. Amid this confusion only Charles Townshend, chancellor of the exchequer, gave any direction to colonial policy, and he died in 1767. Not until the appointment of Lord North as prime minister in 1770 did George find a politician whom he trusted and who also had Parliament's support.

Outside of Parliament, the huge portion of the British nation that was excluded from active participation in politics was stirring as it never had before. Not only was Ireland becoming restless under Britain's continual interference in its affairs, but political corruption in Britain and Parliament's failure to extend either the right to vote or representation to large numbers of British subjects created widespread resentment and led to many calls for reform. Mob rioting in London and elsewhere in England increased dramatically in the 1760s. In 1763, George III noted that there were "insurrections and tumults in every part of the country." By the end of the decade the situation was worse. Lord North was attacked on his way to Parliament; his coach was destroyed and he barely escaped with his life.

Rioting had long been common in England, but many of the popular uprisings of the 1760s were different from those in the past. Far from being limited to particular grievances such as high bread prices, much of the rioting was now directed toward the whole political system. The most important crowd leader was John Wilkes, one of the most colorful demagogues in English history. Wilkes was a member of Parliament and an opposition journalist who in 1763 was arrested and tried for seditiously libeling George III and the government in No. 45 of his newspaper, the *North Briton*. Wilkes immediately became a popular hero, and the cry "Wilkes and Liberty" spread on both sides of the Atlantic. The House of Commons ordered the offensive issue of the newspaper publicly burned, and Wilkes fled to France. In 1768 he returned and was several times elected to the House of Commons, but each time Parliament denied him his seat. London crowds, organized by substantial shopkeepers and artisans, found in Wilkes a symbol of all their pent-up resentments against Britain's corrupt and oligarchic politics. The issue of Wilkes helped to bring together radical reform movements that shook the foundations of Britain's narrow governing class.

Thus in the 1760s and early 1770s the British government was faced with the need to overhaul its empire and gain revenue from its colonies at the very time that the political situation in the British Isles themselves was more chaotic, confused, and disorderly than it had been since the early eighteenth century. No wonder that it took only a bit more than a decade for the whole shaky imperial structure to come crashing down.

The government began its reform of the newly enlarged empire by issuing the Proclamation of 1763. This crown proclamation created three new royal governments—East Florida, West Florida, and Quebec—and enlarged the province of Nova Scotia. It turned the vast trans-Appalachian area into an Indian reservation and prohibited all private individuals from purchasing Indian lands. The aim was to maintain peace in the West and to channel the migration of people northward and southward into the new colonies. There, it was felt, the settlers would be in closer touch with both the mother country and the mercantile system—and more useful as buffers against the Spanish in Louisiana and the remaining French in Canada.

But circumstances destroyed these royal blueprints. Not only were there bewildering shifts of the ministers in charge of the new policy, but news of Pontiac's Indian rebellion in the Ohio Valley in 1763 forced the government to rush its program into effect. The demarcation line along the Appalachians that closed the West to white settlers was hastily and crudely drawn, and some colonists suddenly found themselves living in the Indian reservation. The new trading regulations and sites were widely ignored and created more chaos in the Indian trade than had existed earlier. So confusing was the situation in the West that the British government could never convince the various contending interests that the proclamation was anything more than, in the words of George Washington, who had speculative interests in western lands, "a temporary expedient to quiet the minds of the Indians." Scores of land speculators and lobbyists pressured the unsteady British governments to negotiate a series of Indian treaties shifting the line of settlement westward. But each modification only whetted the appetites of the land speculators and led to some of the most grandiose land schemes in modern history.

In the Quebec Act of 1774, the British government finally tried to steady its dizzy western policy. This act transferred to the province of Quebec the land and control of the Indian trade in the huge area between the Ohio and Mississippi Rivers and allowed Quebec's French inhabitants French law and Roman Catholicism. As enlightened as this act was toward the French Canadians, it managed to anger all American interests—speculators, settlers, and traders alike. This arbitrary alteration of provincial boundaries threatened the security of all colonial boundaries and frightened American Protestants into believing that the British government was trying to erect a hostile Catholic province in the Northwest.

The new colonial trade policies were more coherent than Britain's western policy but no less dangerous in American eyes. The Sugar Act of 1764 was clearly a major successor to the great navigation acts of the late seventeenth century. The series of regulations that it established were designed to tighten the navigation system and in particular to curb the colonists' smuggling and corruption. Absentee customs officials were ordered to return to their posts and were given greater authority and protection. The jurisdiction of the vice-admiralty courts in cases of customs violation was broadened. The navy was granted greater power in inspecting American ships. The use of writs of assistance (or search warrants) was enlarged. To the earlier list of "enumerated" colonial products that had to be exported directly to Britain, such as tobacco and sugar, were added hides, iron, timber, and others. And finally so many more American shippers were required to post bonds and obtain certificates of clearance that nearly all colonial merchants, even those involved only in the coastwise trade, found themselves enmeshed in a bureaucratic web of bonds, certificates, and regulations.

To these frustrating rigidities that were now built into the navigation system were added new customs duties, which raised the expenses of American importers in order to increase British revenue. The Sugar Act imposed duties on foreign cloth, sugar, indigo, coffee, and wine imported into the colonies. More important, the Sugar Act reduced the presumably prohibitory duty of sixpence a gallon on imported foreign West Indian molasses, set by the Molasses Act of 1733, to threepence a gallon. The British government expected that a lower duty on foreign molasses, rigidly enforced, would stop smuggling and lead to the legal importation of foreign molasses and earn money for the crown. The colonists thought otherwise.

These British reforms, which threatened to upset the delicately balanced patterns of trade that had been built up in previous generations, could be regarded as part of Britain's traditional authority over colonial commerce. But the next step in Britain's new imperial program could not be thus regarded; it was radically new. Grenville's ministry, convinced that the customs reforms could not bring in the needed revenue, was determined to try a decidedly different method of extracting American wealth. In March 1765, Parliament by an overwhelming majority passed the Stamp Act, which levied a tax on legal documents, almanacs, newspapers, and nearly every form of paper used in the colonies. Like all duties, the tax was to be paid in British sterling, not in colonial paper money. Although stamp taxes had been used in England since 1694 and several colonial assemblies had resorted to them in the 1750s, Parliament had never before imposed such a tax directly on the colonists.

It is not surprising, therefore, that the Stamp Act galvanized colonial opinion as nothing ever had. "This single stroke," declared William Smith, Jr., of New York, "has lost Great Britain the affection of all her Colonies."

II

AMERICAN RESISTANCE

The atmosphere in the colonies could not have been less receptive to these initial efforts by the British government to reorganize the empire. In the early 1760s, with the curtailing of wartime spending, the earlier commercial boom collapsed. Between 1760 and 1764, American markets were glutted with unsold goods. At the same time, bumper tobacco crops (in part the result of new independent producers) drove tobacco prices down by 75 percent. This economic slump threatened the entire Atlantic credit structure, from London and Scottish merchant houses to small farmers and shopkeepers in the colonies. As a result, business failures and bankruptcies multiplied everywhere.

It is not surprising that the victims of the collapse sought to blame their shifting fortunes on the distant government in England. In fact, the British government's response to the financial crisis could not have been more clumsy and irritating to the Americans. In 1764, Parliament passed a new Currency Act, which prohibited the colonies from issuing paper money as legal tender. This sweeping and simpleminded attempt to solve a complicated problem was only one of the many ways in which British power in these years brought to the surface many deep-rooted antagonisms between the colonies and England.

The Sugar Act, coinciding with this postwar depression, created particularly severe problems for all those who depended on trade with the French and Spanish West Indies. The colonists feared that enforcement of the duty on foreign molasses would ruin the northern rum industry, which in turn would curtail the export trade in fish, foodstuffs, and African slaves to the Caribbean and endanger America's ability to pay for its British imports. These fears, together with hostility to all the new trade regulations accompanying the Sugar Act, stirred up opposition and provoked the first deliberately organized intercolonial protest. In 1764 the assemblies of eight colonies drew up and endorsed formal petitions claiming that the Sugar Act was causing economic injury and sent them to the royal authorities in England.

Not only did royal authorities ignore these petitions, but they went ahead with the Stamp Act of 1765 in the face of mounting colonial objections. This action excited not simply a colonial protest, however, but a firestorm of opposition that swept through the colonies with amazing force. This parliamentary tax, however justifiable it may have been in fiscal terms, posed such a distinct threat to Americans' liberties and the autonomy of their legislatures that they could no longer contain their opposition within the traditional channels of complaints and lobbying.

When word reached America that Parliament had passed the Stamp Act without even considering any of the colonial petitions against it, the colonists reacted angrily. Merchants in the principal ports formed protest associations and pledged to stop importing British goods in order to bring economic pressure on the British government. Newspapers and pamphlets, the number and like of which had never appeared in America before, seethed with resentment against what one New Yorker called "these designing parricides" who had "invited despotism to cross the ocean, and fix her abode in this once happy land." At hastily convened meetings of towns, counties, and legislative assemblies, the colonists' anger boiled over into fiery declarations.

This torrent of angry words could not help but bring the constitutional relationship between Britain and its colonies into question. In the spring of 1765, the Virginia House of Burgesses adopted a series of resolves denouncing the parliamentary taxation and asserting the colonists' right to be taxed only by their elected representatives. These resolves were introduced by Patrick Henry, who at age twenty-nine had just been elected to the legislature. In the dignified setting of the House of Burgesses, Henry dared to repeat his challenge to crown authority that he had earlier made in the Parson's Cause. Just as Julius Caesar had had his Brutus and King Charles I his Oliver Cromwell, so he did not doubt that some American would now stand up for his country against this new tyranny. Henry was stopped by the Speaker of the House for suggesting treason; and some of his resolves (including one proclaiming the right of Virginians to disobey any law that had not been enacted by the Virginia assembly) were too inflammatory to be accepted by the legislature. Nevertheless, colonial newspapers printed the resolves as though the Virginia assembly had endorsed them all. Many Americans became convinced that Virginians had virtually asserted their legislative independence from Great Britain.

Henry's boldness was contagious. The Rhode Island assembly declared the Stamp Act "unconstitutional" and authorized the colony's officials to ignore it. In October 1765 thirty-seven delegates from nine colonies met in New York in the Stamp Act Congress and drew up a set of formal declarations and petitions denying Parliament's right to tax them. But as remarkable as this unprecedented display of colonial unity was, the Stamp Act Congress, with its opening acknowledgment of "all due Subordination to that August Body the Parliament of Great Britain," could not fully express American hostility.

Ultimately it was mob violence that destroyed the Stamp Act in America. On August 14, 1765, a crowd tore apart the office and attacked the home of Andrew Oliver, the stamp distributor for Massachusetts. The next day Oliver promised not to enforce the Stamp Act. As news of the rioting spread to other colonies, similar violence and threats of violence spread with it. From Newport, Rhode Island, to Charleston, South Carolina, local groups organized for resistance. In many places fire and artillery companies, artisan associations, and other fraternal bodies formed the basis for these emerging local organizations, which commonly called themselves

Sons of Liberty. Led mostly by members of the middle ranks—shopkeepers, printers, master mechanics, small merchants—these Sons of Liberty burned effigies of royal officials, forced stamp agents to resign, compelled businessmen and judges to carry on without stamps, developed an intercolonial network of correspondence, generally enforced nonimportation of British goods, and managed antistamp activities throughout the colonies.

BRITISH REACTION

In England the Rockingham Whigs (who had been critical of the policies of George III and Grenville) were now in charge of the ministry, and the government was prepared to retreat. Not only were these Whigs eager to disavow Grenville's policies, but they had close connections with British merchants who had been hurt by American economic boycotts. In February 1766, Parliament repealed the Stamp Act.

Despite the British government's attempt to offset its repeal of the Stamp Act by a declaration that Parliament had the right to legislate for the colonies "in all cases whatsoever," after 1765 the imperial relationship and American respect for British authority—indeed, for all authority—would never be the same. The crisis over the Stamp Act aroused and unified Americans as no previous political event ever had. It stimulated bold political and constitutional writings throughout the colonies, deepened the colonists' political consciousness and participation, and produced new forms of organized popular resistance. In their mobs the people learned that they could compel both the resignation of royal officials and obedience to other popular measures. Through "their riotous meetings," Governor Horatio Sharpe of Maryland observed in 1765, the people "begin to think they can by the same way of proceeding accomplish anything their leaders may tell them they ought to do."

The British government could not rely on a simple declaration of parliamentary supremacy to satisfy its continuing need for more revenue. Since the colonists evidently would not stomach a "direct" and "internal" tax like the stamp tax, British officials concluded that the government would have to gather revenue through the more traditional "indirect" and "external" customs duties. After all, the colonists were already paying duties on molasses, wine, and several other imported products as a result of the Sugar Act. Consequently, in 1767, led by Chancellor of the Exchequer Charles Townshend, Parliament imposed new levies on glass, paint, paper, and tea imported into the colonies. Although all the new customs duties, particularly the lowered molasses duty of 1766, began bringing in an average yearly revenue of £45,000—in contrast to only £2,000 a year collected before 1764—the yearly sums that were raised were scarcely a tenth of the annual cost of maintaining the army in America.

Convinced that something more drastic had to be done, the British government reorganized the executive authority of the empire. In 1767–68 the government created the American Board of Customs, located in Boston and reporting directly to the Treasury. It also established three new superior vice-admiralty courts—in Boston, Philadelphia, and Charleston—to supplement the one already in operation in Halifax, Nova Scotia. In belated recognition of the importance of the colonies, it created a new secretaryship of state exclusively for American affairs, an office that would cap the entire structure of colonial government. At the same time, the government decided to economize by pulling back much of its army from its costly deployment in the West and by closing many remote posts. The army was now to be stationed in the coastal cities, where, according to Parliament's Quartering Act of 1765, the colonists would be responsible for its housing and supply. Not only did this withdrawal of the troops eastward away from the French and Indians contribute to the chaos in the western territory, but the concentration of a standing army in peacetime amid a civilian population blurred the army's original mission in America and raised the colonists' fears of British intentions.

By 1768 there was a new determination among royal officials to put down the unruly forces that seemed to be loose everywhere. Amid the ministerial squabbling of the late 1760s, some officials were suggesting that British troops be used against American rioters. Revenue from the Townshend duties was earmarked for the salaries of royal officials in the colonies so that they would be independent of the colonial legislatures. The colonial governors were instructed to maintain tight control of the assemblies and not to agree to acts that would increase popular representation in the assemblies or the length of time the legislatures sat. Royal officials toyed with more elaborate plans for remodeling the colonial governments: Some proposed that the Massachusetts charter be revoked; others, that royal councils, or upper houses, be strengthened. Some even suggested introducing a titled nobility into America to sit in these colonial upper houses.

DEEPENING OF THE CRISIS

In the atmosphere of the late 1760s, these measures and proposals were not simply irritating; they were explosive. After the Stamp Act crisis, American sensitivities to all forms of English taxation were thoroughly aroused. With the passage of the Townshend duties, the earlier pattern of resistance reappeared and expanded. Pamphleteers and newspaper writers again leaped to the defense of American liberties. The wealthy, cultivated Philadelphia lawyer John Dickinson, in his *Letters from a Farmer in Pennsylvania* (1767–68), the most popular pamphlet of the 1760s, rejected all parliamentary taxation. According to Dickinson, Parliament had no right to impose either "internal" or "external" taxes levied for the sole purpose of raising revenue. He called for the revival of the nonimportation agreements that had been so effective in the resistance to the Stamp Act.

Following Boston's lead in March 1768, merchants in colonial ports again formed associations to boycott British goods. Despite much competition among different groups of merchants and jealousy among the ports, by 1769–70 these nonimportation agreements had cut British sales to the northern colonies by nearly two thirds. The colonists encouraged the wearing of homespun cloth, and in New England villages "Daughters of Liberty" held spinning bees. By now more Americans were involved in the resistance movement. Extralegal groups and committees, usually but not always restrained by popular leaders, emerged to intimidate tobacco inspectors in Maryland, punish importers in Philadelphia, mob a publisher in Boston, and harass customs officials in New York.

Nowhere were events more spectacular than in Massachusetts. There the situation was so inflammatory that every move triggered a string of explosions that widened the chasm between the colonists and royal authority. Forty-six-year-old Samuel Adams, with his puritanical zeal, organizational skill, and deep hatred of crown authority, emerged as a dominant political figure. It was later said that 1768 was the year Adams decided on independence for America. Given the events in Massachusetts during that year, it is easy to see why.

In February 1768 the Massachusetts House of Representatives issued to the other colonial legislatures a "circular letter" that denounced the Townshend duties as unconstitutional violations of the principle of no taxation without representation. Lord Hillsborough, the secretary of state of the newly created American Department and a hard-liner on controlling the colonies, ordered the Massachusetts House to revoke its circular letter. When the House defied this order by a majority of 92 to 17 (thereby enshrining the number 92 in patriot rituals), Governor Francis Bernard dissolved the Massachusetts assembly. With this legal means for dealing with grievances silenced, mobs and other unauthorized groups in the colony broke out in violence. Boston, which was rapidly becoming a symbol of colonial resistance, ordered its inhabitants to arm and called for a convention of town delegates—a meeting that would have no legal standing. Attacked by mobs, customs officials in Boston found it impossible to enforce the navigation regulations and pleaded for military help. When a British warship arrived in Boston in June 1768, emboldened customs officials promptly seized John Hancock's ship *Liberty* for violating the trade acts. Since the wealthy Hancock was prominently associated with the resistance movement, the seizure was intended to be an object lesson in royal authority. Its effect, however, was to set off one of the fiercest riots in Boston's history.

Hillsborough, believing that Massachusetts was in a state of virtual anarchy, dispatched two regiments of troops from Ireland. They began arriving in Boston on October 1, 1768, and their appearance marked a crucial turning point in the escalating controversy: For the first time the British government had sent a substantial number of soldiers to enforce British authority in the colonies. By 1769 there were nearly 4,000 armed redcoats in the crowded seaport of 15,000 inhabitants. Since the colonists shared traditional English fears of standing armies, relations between townspeople and soldiers deteriorated. On March 5, 1770, a party of eight harassed British soldiers fired on a threatening crowd and killed five civilians. The "Boston Massacre," especially as it was depicted in Paul Revere's exaggerated engraving, aroused American passions and inspired some of the most sensational rhetoric heard in the Revolutionary era.

This resort to troops to quell disorder was the ultimate symptom of the ineffectiveness of the British government's authority, and many Britons knew it. The use of force, it was argued in Parliament and in the administration itself, only destroyed the goodwill on which the colonists' relation to the mother country must ultimately rest. Indeed, throughout the escalation of events in the 1760s, many British ministers remained confused and uncertain. "There is the most urgent reason to do what is right, and immediately," wrote Secretary at War Lord Barrington to Governor Bernard in 1767, "but what is that right and who is to do it?" English officials advanced and retreated, pleaded and threatened, in ever more desperate efforts to enforce British authority without aggravating the colonists' hostility. In the winter of 1767–68 the British responded to the disorder in Massachusetts with a series of parliamentary resolutions in which they condemned Massachusetts's denial of parliamentary supremacy and threatened to bring the colonial offenders to England for trial. Yet strong minority opposition in the House of Commons and the ministry's unwillingness to bring on further crises made these resolutions empty gestures: The government was now only waging what one Englishman called "a paper war with the colonies."

By the end of the 1760s, British plans for reorganizing the empire were in shambles. Colonial legislatures and royal governors were at loggerheads. Colonial papers daily denounced Britain's authority, and mobs were becoming increasingly common in the countryside as well as in city streets. Customs officials, under continual intimidation, quarreled with merchants, naval officers, and royal governors. The customs officials' entanglement in local politics made efficient or evenhanded enforcement of the trade acts impossible. What enforcement there was thus appeared arbitrary and discriminatory, and drove many merchants, such as the wealthy South Carolinian Henry Laurens, who had earlier been contemptuous of the Sons of Liberty, into bitter opposition.

The financial returns to the British government from the customs reforms seemed in no way worth the costs. By 1770 less than £21,000 had been collected from the Townshend duties, while the loss to British business because of American nonimportation movements during the previous year was put at £700,000. It was therefore not surprising that the British government now abandoned the hope of securing revenue from the duties and labeled the Townshend program, in Lord

Hillsborough's words, "contrary to the true principles of commerce." In 1770, after years of chaos in the British government, the reorganization of the king's ministry under Lord North prepared the way for repeal of the Townshend duties. Only the duty on tea was retained, to serve, as Lord North said, "as a mark of the supremacy of Parliament, and an efficient declaration of their right to govern the colonies."

Yet the stabilization of English politics that came with the formation of North's ministry and the repeal of the Townshend duties could scarcely undo what had already been done. Whatever ties of affection had earlier existed between the colonists and Great Britain were fast being destroyed by irritation and suspicion. Many Americans were coming to believe that their interests and their hopes, their rights and their liberties, were threatened by British power. Although politicians on both sides of the Atlantic were by the early 1770s calling for a return to the conditions that had existed before 1763, going back was clearly no longer possible.

For two years there was a superficial tranquility. Then the struggle began again. In 1772, Rhode Islanders, angry at the heavy-handed enforcement of the navigation acts, boarded the British naval schooner *Gaspée*, which had run aground in Narragansett Bay, sank it, and wounded its captain. A royal commission, empowered to send all suspects to England for trial, was dispatched from England to inquire into the sinking. This authority seemed to fulfill earlier British threats to bypass regular judicial procedures, and it provoked Virginia into calling for the creation of intercolonial committees of correspondence, to which five assemblies responded.

Under Boston's and particularly Samuel Adams's leadership, Massachusetts towns had already begun organizing committees of correspondence. In the fall of 1772, Bostonians published a fiery document, *The Votes and Proceedings* of their town meeting, which listed all the British violations of American rights. These included taxing and legislating for the colonists without their consent, introducing standing armies in peacetime, extending the powers of vice-admiralty courts (which did not use jury trials), restricting colonial manufacturing, and threatening to establish Anglican bishops in America. The publication was sent to the 260 towns of Massachusetts, and more than half responded positively in the greatest outpouring of ordinary local opinion the resistance movement had yet seen. By the end of 1773, independence was being discussed freely in colonial newspapers. Since the North government was determined to uphold the sovereignty of Parliament, an eventual confrontation seemed unavoidable.

In 1773, Parliament provided the occasion for a confrontation by granting the East India Company the exclusive privilege of selling tea in America. Although the North government intended this Tea Act only to be a means of saving the East India Company from bankruptcy, it set off the final series of explosions. For the act not only allowed colonial radicals to draw attention once again to the unconstitutionality of the existing tax on tea, but it also permitted the company to grant monopolies for selling tea to favored colonial merchants—a provision that angered those American traders who were excluded. The Tea Act spread an alarm throughout the colonies. In several ports colonists stopped the ships from landing the company's tea. When tea ships in Boston were prevented from unloading their cargoes, Governor Thomas Hutchinson, whose merchant family had been given the right to sell tea, refused to allow the ships to leave without landing the tea. In response, on December 16, 1773, a group of patriots disguised as Indians dumped about £10,000 worth of tea into Boston Harbor. "This is the most magnificent movement of all," exulted John Adams, an ambitious young lawyer from Braintree, Massachusetts. "This destruction of the tea is so bold, so daring, so firm, intrepid, and inflexible, and it must have so important consequences, and so lasting, that I can't but consider it an epocha in history."

Adams was right. To the British the Boston Tea Party was

the ultimate outrage. Angry officials and many of the politically active people in Great Britain clamored for a punishment that would squarely confront America with the issue of Parliament's right to legislate for the colonies. "We are now to establish our authority," Lord North told the House of Commons, "or give it up entirely." In 1774, Parliament passed a succession of laws that came to be known as the Coercive Acts. The first of these closed the port of Boston until the destroyed tea was paid for. The second altered the Massachusetts charter and reorganized the government: Members of the Council, or upper house, were now to be appointed by the royal governor rather than elected by the legislature, town meetings were restricted, and the governor's power of appointing judges and sheriffs was strengthened. The third act allowed royal officials who had been charged with capital offenses to be tried in England or in another colony to avoid hostile juries. The fourth gave the governor power to take over private buildings for the quartering of troops instead of using barracks. At the same time, Thomas Gage, commander in chief of the British army in America, was made governor of the colony of Massachusetts.

These Coercive Acts were the last straw. They convinced Americans once and for all that Parliament had no more right to make laws for them than to tax them.

THE IMPERIAL DEBATE

The colonists had been groping toward this denial of Parliament's power from the beginning of the controversy. For a decade they had engaged in a remarkable constitutional debate with the British over the nature of public power, representation, and the empire. This debate exposed for the first time just how divergent America's previous political experience had been from that of the mother country.

With the passage of the Stamp Act, Parliament's first unmistakable tax levy on Americans, American intellectual resistance was immediately raised to the highest plane of principle. "It is inseparably essential to the freedom of a people, and the undoubted rights of Englishmen," the Stamp Act Congress declared in 1765, "that no taxes should be imposed on them, but with their own consent, given personally, or by their representatives." And since "the people of these colonies are not, and from their local circumstances, cannot be represented in the House of Commons in Great Britain," the colonists would be represented and taxed only by persons who were known and chosen by themselves and who served in their respective legislatures. This statement defined the American position at the outset of the controversy, and despite subsequent confusion and stumbling, the colonists never abandoned this essential point.

Once the British ministry sensed a stirring of colonial opposition to the Stamp Act, a number of English government pamphleteers set out to explain and justify Parliament's taxation of the colonies. Although the arguments of these writers differed, they all eventually agreed that Americans, like Englishmen everywhere, were subject to acts of Parliament through a system of "virtual" representation. These writers argued that it was this concept of virtual representation, as distinct from actual representation, that gave Parliament its supreme authority—its sovereignty. One government pamphleteer wrote that even though the colonists, like "nine-tenths of the people of Britain," did not in fact choose any representative to the House of Commons, they were undoubtedly "a part, and an important part of the Commons of Great Britain: they are represented in Parliament in the same manner as those inhabitants of Britain are who have not voices in elections."

During the eighteenth century the British electorate made up only a tiny proportion of the nation; probably only one in six British adult males had the right to vote, compared with two out of three in America. In addition, Britain's electoral districts were a confusing mixture of sizes and shapes left over from centuries of history. Some of the constituencies were large, with thousands of voters, but others were small and more or less in the pocket of a single great landowner. Many of the electoral districts had few voters, and some so-called rotten boroughs had no inhabitants at all. One town, Dunwich, continued to send representatives to Parliament even though it had long since slipped into the North Sea. At the same time, some of England's largest cities, such as Manchester and Birmingham, which had grown suddenly in the mid eighteenth century, sent no representatives to Parliament. Although radical reformers, among them John Wilkes, increasingly criticized this jumbled political structure, parliamentary reform was slow in coming and would not begin until 1832. Many Englishmen, as did Edmund Burke in 1774, justified this hodgepodge of representation by claiming that each member of Parliament represented the whole British nation, and not just the particular locality he came from. According to this view, people were represented in England not by the process of election, which was considered incidental to representation, but rather by the mutual interests that members of Parliament were presumed to share with all Englishmen for whom they spoke—including those, like the colonists, who did not actually vote for them.

The Americans immediately and strongly rejected these British claims that they were "virtually" represented in the same way that the nonvoters of cities like Manchester and Birmingham were. In the most notable colonial pamphlet written in opposition to the Stamp Act, *Considerations on the Propriety of Imposing Taxes* (1765), Daniel Dulany of Maryland admitted the relevance in England of virtual representation, but he denied its applicability to America. For America, he wrote, was a distinct community from England and thus could hardly be represented by members of Parliament with whom it had no common interests. Others pushed beyond Dulany's argument, however, and challenged the very idea of virtual representation. If the people were to be properly represented in a legislature, many colonists said, not only did they have to vote directly for the members of the legislature, but they also had to be represented by members whose numbers were proportionate to the size of the population they spoke for. What purpose is served, asked James Otis of Massachusetts in 1765, by the continual attempts of Englishmen to justify the lack of American representation in Parliament by citing the examples of Manchester and Birmingham, which returned no members to the House of Commons? "If those now so considerable places are not represented, they ought to be."

In the New World, electoral districts were not the products of history that stretched back centuries, but rather were recent and regular creations that were related to changes in population. When new towns in Massachusetts and new counties in Virginia were formed, new representatives customarily were sent to the respective colonial legislatures. As a consequence, many Americans had come to believe in a very different kind of representation from that of the English. Their belief in "actual" representation made the process of election not incidental but central to representation. Actual representation stressed the closest possible connection between the local electors and their representatives. For Americans it was only proper that representatives be residents of the localities they spoke for and that people of the locality have the right to instruct their representatives. Americans thought it only fair that localities be represented more or less in proportion to their population. In short, the American belief in actual representation pointed toward the fullest and most equal participation of the people in the process of government that the modern world had ever seen.

Yet while Americans were denying Parliament's right to tax them because they were not represented in the House of Commons, they knew that Parliament had exercised some authority over their affairs during the previous century. They therefore tried to explain what that authority should be. What was the "due subordination" that the Stamp Act Congress admitted Americans owed Parliament? Could the colonists accept parliamentary legislation but not taxation? Could they accept "external" customs duties for the purpose of regulating trade, but not "internal" stamp taxes for the purpose of raising revenue? In his famous *Letters from a Farmer in Pennsylvania,* John Dickinson rejected the idea that Parliament could rightly impose "external" or "internal" taxes and made clear that the colonists opposed all forms of parliamentary taxation. But Dickinson recognized that the empire required some sort of central regulatory authority, particularly for commerce, and conceded Parliament's supervisory legislative power so far as it preserved "the connection between the several parts of the British empire." The empire, it seemed to many colonists, was a unified body for some affairs but not for others.

To counter all these halting and fumbling efforts by the colonists to divide parliamentary authority, the British offered a simple but powerful argument. Since they could not conceive of the empire as anything but a single, unified community, they found absurd and meaningless all these American distinctions between trade regulations and taxation, between "external" and "internal" taxes, and between separate spheres of authority. If Parliament even "in one instance" was as supreme over the colonists as it was over the people of England, wrote a subcabinet official, William Knox, in 1769, then the Americans were members "of the same community with the people of England." On the other hand, if Parliament's authority over the colonists was denied "in any particular," then it must be denied in "all instances," and the union between Great Britain and the colonies must be dissolved. "There is no alternative," Knox concluded. "Either the colonies are part of the community of Great Britain or they are in a state of nature with respect to her, and in no case can be subject to the jurisdiction of that legislative power which represents her community, which is the British Parliament."

What made this British argument so powerful was its basis in the widely accepted doctrine of sovereignty—the belief that in every state there could be only one final, indivisible, and uncontestable supreme authority. This was the most important concept of eighteenth-century English political theory, and it became the issue over which the empire was finally broken.

This idea that, in the end, every state had to have one single supreme undivided law-making authority had been the basis of the British position from the beginning. The British expressed this concept of sovereignty officially in the Declaratory Act of 1766, which, following the repeal of the Stamp Act, affirmed Parliament's authority to make laws binding the colonists "in all cases whatsoever." It was natural for the British to locate sovereignty in Parliament, for it was the institution to which they paid the greatest respect. Indeed, it would be difficult to exaggerate the veneration felt by metropolitan Britons toward their Parliament. All good Britons could be suspicious of crown power but not of Parliament. Parliament had always been the bulwark of their liberties, their protector against crown abuses.

The colonists could never share this traditional reverence toward Parliament, and on this issue they inevitably parted from their fellow Englishmen, not by rejecting the doctrine of sovereignty but by relocating it. In 1773, Massachusetts Governor Thomas Hutchinson was provoked into directly challenging the radical movement and its belief in the limited nature of Parliament's power. In a dramatic and well-publicized speech to the Massachusetts legislature, Hutchinson attempted once and for all to clarify the central constitutional issue between America and Great Britain and to show the colonists how unreasonable their views were. "I know of no line," he declared, "that can be drawn between the supreme authority of

Parliament and the total independence of the colonies, as it is impossible there should be two independent legislatures in one and the same state."

By 1773 many Americans despaired of trying to divide what royal officials told them could not be divided. The Massachusetts House of Representatives had a simple answer to Hutchinson's position. If, as Governor Hutchinson had said, there was no middle ground between the supreme authority of Parliament and the total independence of the colonies from Parliament, the House members felt that there could be no doubt that "we were thus independent." The logic of sovereignty therefore forced a fundamental shift in the American position.

By 1774 the leading colonists, including Thomas Jefferson and John Adams, were arguing that only the separate American legislatures were sovereign in America. According to this argument, Parliament had no final authority over America, and the colonies were connected to the empire only through the king. The most the colonists would concede was that Parliament had the right to regulate their external commerce only "from the necessity of the case, and a regard to the mutual interest of both countries," as the *Declarations and Resolves of the First Continental Congress* put it. But the British government remained committed to parliamentary sovereignty embodied in the Declaratory Act, which no American leader could any longer take seriously.

It was now only a matter of time before these irreconcilable positions led to armed conflict.

III

REVOLUTION

By 1774, within the short span of a decade following the introduction of the imperial reforms, Americans who had celebrated George III's coronation were in virtual rebellion against Great Britain. During the two years after the Coercive Acts of 1774, events moved rapidly, and reconciliation between Britain and its colonies became increasingly unlikely. By this time the crisis had become more than a simple breakdown in the imperial relationship. The colonists' extraordinary efforts to understand what was happening transformed their resistance and ultimately their rebellion into a world-historical revolution. The Americans' Declaration of Independence in 1776 turned their separation from Britain into an event that many Americans and some Europeans believed was unprecedented in human history. Americans saw themselves striving not only to make themselves free, but also to bring freedom to the whole world.

THE APPROACH TO INDEPENDENCE

The Coercive Acts of 1774 provoked open rebellion in America. Not only had the abuses of the English government aroused the Americans' principles, but repeated expressions of English arrogance had finally worn out their tempers. Whatever royal authority was left in the colonies now dissolved. Many local communities, with a freedom they had not had since the seventeenth century, attempted to put together new popular governments from the bottom up. Mass meetings that sometimes attracted thousands of aroused colonists endorsed resolutions and called for new political organizations. Committees of different sizes and names—committees of safety, of inspection, of merchants, of mechanics—competed with one another for political control.

In the various colonies royal government was displaced in a variety of ways, depending on how extensive and personal previous royal authority had been. In Massachusetts, where the crown's authority had reached into the villages and towns through the royally appointed justices of the peace, the displacement was greater than in Virginia, where royal influence had scarcely touched the control of the counties by the powerful landowners. But everywhere there was a fundamental transfer of authority that opened new opportunities for new men to assert themselves.

By the end of 1774, in many of the colonies local associations were controlling and regulating various aspects of American life. Committees manipulated voters, directed appointments, organized the militia, managed trade, intervened between creditors and debtors, levied taxes, issued licenses, and supervised or closed the courts. Royal governors stood by in helpless amazement as new informal governments gradually grew up around them. These new governments ranged from town and county committees and the newly created provincial congresses to a general congress of the colonies— the First Continental Congress, which convened in Philadelphia in September 1774.

In all, fifty-five delegates from twelve colonies (all except Georgia) participated in the First Continental Congress. Some colonists, and even some royal officials, hoped that this Congress might work to reestablish imperial authority. Those who were eager to break the bond with Great Britain, however, won the first round. Led by the cousins Samuel and John Adams from Massachusetts, and by Patrick Henry and Richard Henry Lee from Virginia, the Congress endorsed the fiery Resolves of Suffolk County, Massachusetts, which recommended outright resistance to the Coercive Acts. But the Congress was not yet ready for independence. It came very close—failing by the vote of a single colony—to considering further and perhaps adopting a plan of union between Britain and the colonies proposed by Joseph Galloway, leader of the Pennsylvania assembly and spokesman for the conservative congressional delegates from the middle colonies. Galloway's plan was radical enough: It called for the creation of a grand colonial council composed of representatives from each colony. Laws passed by either the American grand council or the British Parliament were to be subject to mutual review and approval.

By 1774, however, it was unlikely, even if Galloway's plan had been adopted, that the Congress could have reversed the transfer of authority that was taking place in the colonies. In the end, the Continental Congress simply recognized the new local authorities in American politics and gave them its blessing by establishing the Continental Association. This continentwide organization put into effect the nonimportation, nonexportation, and nonconsumption of goods that the Congress had agreed on. Committees in all the counties, cities, and towns were now ordered by the Congress "attentively to observe the conduct of all persons," to condemn publicly all violators as "enemies of American liberty," and to "break off all dealings" with them.

Thus with the Congress's endorsement of the Continental Association, local committees, speaking in the name of "the body of the people," carried on the political transformation. Groups of men, from a few dozen to several thousand, marched through villages and city streets searching out enemies of the people. Suspected enemies, under threat of being tarred and feathered, were often forced to take back unfriendly words or designs against the public, to sign confessions of guilt and repentance, and to swear new oaths of friendship to the people. In all the colonies there were signs of an emerging new political order.

These remarkable political changes were not simply the product of the colonists' resistance to British imperial reform. Britain's attempts to reorganize its empire took place not in a vacuum, but in complicated, highly charged situations existing in each colony. In some cases these local political conditions had as much to do with the escalation of the controversy between the colonies and the mother country as did the steps taken by the British government three thousand miles away. Everywhere in the 1760s various groups in the colonies were eager to exploit popular resentment against the British reforms in order to gain local political advantage—with, however, little understanding of the ultimate consequences of their actions.

In New York, for example, political factions that were led by the well-to-do Livingston and De Lancey families vied with each other in whipping up opposition to the imperial legislation and in winning the support of popular extralegal groups such as the Sons of Liberty. Thus these gentry generally helped expand the rights and participation of the people in politics—not with the aim of furthering electoral democracy, but only for the tactical purpose of gaining control of the elective assemblies. While this sort of unplanned popularization of politics had gone on in the past, particularly in urban areas, the inflamed atmosphere generated by the imperial crisis gave it a new explosive power with unpredictable implications.

In colony after colony local and often long-standing quarrels became so entangled with imperial antagonisms that they reinforced one another in a spiraling momentum that brought all governmental authority into question. Even authorities in those colonies that were not ruled by royal governors, such as the proprietary governments of Pennsylvania and Maryland, were victimized by the imperial crisis. Thus in Maryland in 1770 a proclamation by the proprietary governor setting the fees that were paid to government officials seemed to violate the principle of no taxation without representation that had been made so vivid by the imperial debate. This executive proclamation provoked a bitter local struggle that forced Daniel Dulany, a wealthy member of the colony's council and former opponent of the Stamp Act, into defending the governor. In the end, the controversy destroyed the governor's capacity to rule and made Dulany a loyalist to the British cause.

By the 1770s all these developments, without anyone's clearly intending it, were creating a new kind of popular politics in America. The rhetoric of liberty now brought to the surface long-latent political tendencies. Ordinary people were no longer willing to trust only wealthy and learned gentlemen to represent them in government. Various artisan, religious, and ethnic groups now felt that their particular interests were so distinct that only people of their own kind could speak for them. In 1774 radicals in Philadelphia demanded that seven artisans and six Germans be added to the revolutionary committee of the city.

Americans today are used to such "coalition" and "interest-group" politics, but their eighteenth-century counterparts were not. Educated gentlemen such as the prominent Oxford-trained landowner William Henry Drayton of South Carolina complained of having to participate in government with men who knew only "how to cut up a beast in the market" or "to cobble an old shoe." "Nature never intended that such men should be profound politicians, or able statesmen." In 1775 the royal governor of Georgia noted in astonishment that the committee in control of Savannah consisted of "a Parcel of the Lowest People, chiefly carpenters, shoemakers, Blacksmiths etc. with a Jew at their head." In some colonies politicians called for an expanded suffrage, the use of the ballot rather than the customary oral voting, the opening of legislative meetings to the public, the printing of legislative minutes, and the recording of votes taken in the legislatures. All these proposals enlarged the political arena and limited the power of those who clung to the traditional ways of private arrangements and personal influence.

Everywhere in the colonies "incendiaries" (as royal officials called them) used fiery popular rhetoric and competed openly for political leadership. More and more "new men" took advantage of the people's resentments of the British regulations and actively campaigned for popular election in order to bypass the traditional narrow and patronage-controlled channels of politics. The political atmosphere in America was now charged as never before with both deep animosities and new hopes for bettering the world. Americans told themselves they were "on the eve of some great and unusual events," events that "may form a new era, and give a new turn to human affairs."

Men who, like Thomas Hutchinson, had been reared in the old ways and had benefited from them stood bewildered and helpless in the face of these popularizing developments. They possessed neither the psychological capacity nor the political sensitivity to understand—let alone to deal with—this popular politics and the moral outrage and fiery zeal that lay behind it. They intrigued and schemed, and they tried to manipulate those who they thought were the important people in the opposition. (In 1768, for example, John Adams was offered the office of advocate-general in the Massachusetts admiralty court.) When they could not buy them off, they accused those individuals of demagoguery or ridiculed them as upstarts. Frightened by the increased violence, they struck out furiously at the kinds of popular politics they believed were undermining authority and causing the violence. Traditional and prudent men of this sort could not accept a new and different world, and soon they either fell silent or became loyalists, determined to remain faithful to the king and to support the hierarchical society that had bred them.

THE DECLARATION OF INDEPENDENCE

By the beginning of 1775 the British government was already preparing for military action. By this time North's supporters and the king himself saw no choice but force to bring the colonists back into line. As early as November 1774, George III had told North that "blows must decide whether they are to be subject to the Country or Independent." The British government thus built up its army and navy and began restraining the commerce first of New England and then of the other colonies.

In May 1775 delegates from the colonies met in Philadelphia for the Second Continental Congress, to take up where the first Congress had left off. Outwardly the Congress continued the policy of resolves and reconciliation. In July, at the urging of John Dickinson, the Congress approved the Olive Branch Petition, which claimed loyalty to the king and humbly asked him to break with his "artful and cruel" ministers, whom the Congress blamed for the oppressive measures. At the same time, the Congress issued a Declaration of the Causes and Necessities of Taking Up Arms (largely written by Dickinson and Thomas Jefferson) in which it denied that Americans had any "ambitious design of separating from Great Britain, and establishing independent states." As this superb summary of the American case against Britain demonstrated, the time for paper solutions had passed.

In April 1775 fighting had broken out in Massachusetts. Since the British government had long assumed that Boston was the center of the disturbances in America, it believed that isolating and punishing that port city would essentially undermine all colonial resistance. The Coercive Acts of 1774 had rested on this assumption, and the British military actions of 1775 were simply a logical extension of the same assumption. The British government, thinking that it was dealing only with mobs led by a few seditious instigators, therefore ordered its commander in Massachusetts, General Gage, to arrest the rebel leaders, to break up their bases, and to reassert royal authority in the colony. On April 18–19, 1775, Gage's army attempted to seize rebel arms and ammunition stored at Concord, a town northwest of Boston. Colonial scouts, including the silversmith Paul Revere, rode ahead of the advancing redcoats, warned patriot leaders John Hancock and Samuel Adams to flee, and roused the farmers of the countryside—the minutemen—to arms. No one knows who fired first at Lexington, but shots between the colonial militia and British troops were exchanged there and later at nearby Concord, where the British found only a few supplies.

During their long march back to Boston, the strung-out British columns were repeatedly harassed by patriot militia. By the end of the day, 273 redcoats and 95 patriots had been killed or wounded, and the countryside was aflame with revolt. From positions in Charlestown and Dorchester, the colonists quickly surrounded the besieged British in Boston and thus raised doubts among the British authorities that police action would be enough to quell the rebellion.

Two months later, in June 1775, British soldiers attempted to dislodge the American fortification on a spur of Bunker Hill in Charlestown, overlooking Boston. The British assumed, as one of their generals, John Burgoyne, put it, that no numbers of "untrained rabble" could ever stand up against "trained troops." Under General William Howe, British forces attempted a series of frontal assaults on the American position. These attacks were eventually successful, but only at the terrible cost of 1,000 British casualties—more than 40 percent of Howe's troops. At Bunker Hill—the first formal battle of the Revolution—the British suffered their heaviest losses in what would become a long and bloody war. "Never had the British Army so ungenerous an enemy to oppose," declared a British soldier in the aftermath of Bunker Hill. The American riflemen "conceal themselves behind trees etc till an opportunity presents itself of taking a shot at our advance sentries, which done they immediately retreat. What an unfair method of carrying on a war!"

When news of the fighting reached Philadelphia, the Second Continental Congress had to assume the responsibilities of a central government for the colonies. The Congress created the Continental Army, appointed George Washington of Virginia as commander, issued paper money for the support of colonial troops, and formed a committee to negotiate with foreign countries. The Americans were preparing to wage war against the greatest power of the eighteenth century.

By the summer of 1775 the escalation of actions and reactions was out of control. On August 23, George III, ignoring the colonists' Olive Branch Petition, proclaimed the colonies in open rebellion. In October he publicly accused them of aiming at independence. By December 1775 the British government had declared all American shipping liable to seizure by British warships. As early as May 1775, American forces had captured Fort Ticonderoga at the head of Lake Champlain. In an effort to bring the Canadians into the struggle against Britain, the Congress ordered makeshift forces under Richard Montgomery and Benedict Arnold to invade Canada, but the colonists were badly defeated in Quebec in the winter of 1775–76. With all this fighting between Britain and its colonies taking place, it was only a matter of time before the Americans formally cut the remaining ties to Great Britain. Although no official American body had as yet endorsed independence, the idea was obviously in the air.

It was left to Thomas Paine, a former English corsetmaker, schoolmaster, and twice-dismissed excise officer who had only arrived in the colonies in late 1774, to express in January 1776 the accumulated American rage against George III. In his pamphlet *Common Sense,* Paine dismissed the king as the "Royal Brute" and called for American independence immediately. "For God's sake, let us come to a final separation ...," he implored. "The birthday of a new world is at hand."

Common Sense was the most incendiary and popular pamphlet of the entire Revolutionary era; it went through twenty-five editions in 1776 alone. In it Paine rejected the traditional and stylized forms of persuasion designed for educated gentlemen and reached out for new readers among the artisan- and tavern-centered worlds of the cities. Unlike more genteel writers, Paine did not decorate his pamphlet with Latin quotations and learned references to the literature of Western culture, but instead relied on his readers knowing only the Bible and the *Book of Common Prayer*. Although Paine was criticized for using ungrammatical language and coarse imagery, he showed the common people, who in the past had not been very involved in politics, that fancy words and Latin quotations no longer mattered as much as honesty and sincerity and the natural revelation of feelings.

In the early spring of 1776 the Congress opened America's ports to all foreign trade, authorized the outfitting of privateers to prey on America's enemies, and prepared for independence. On July 4, 1776, the delegates formally approved the Declaration of Independence, a thirteen-hundred-word document largely written by the graceful hand of Thomas Jefferson of Virginia. In the Declaration the king, who was now regarded as the only remaining link between the colonists and Great Britain, was held accountable for every grievance that the Americans had suffered since 1763. The reign of George III, Americans declared "to a candid world," was "a history of repeated injuries and usurpations, all having in direct object the establishment of an absolute Tyranny over these States."

Congress removed a quarter of Jefferson's original draft, including a passage that blamed George III for the horrors of the slave trade. As Jefferson later recalled, South Carolina and Georgia objected to the passage, and some northern delegates were also a "little tender" on the subject, "for though their people have very few slaves themselves yet they had been pretty considerable carriers."

Indeed, all the colonists had long been implicated in African slavery. Of the total American population of 2.5 million in 1776, one fifth—500,000 men, women, and children—was enslaved. Virginia had the most slaves—200,000, or 40 percent of its population. Although most of the slaves were held by southerners, slavery was not inconsequential in the North. Fourteen percent of New York's population was enslaved. New Jersey and Rhode Island held 8 percent and 6 percent of their populations, respectively, in lifetime hereditary bondage. Slavery was a national institution, and nearly every white American directly or indirectly benefited from it. By 1776, however, nearly every American leader knew that its continued existence violated everything the Revolution was about.

Despite the failure of the Declaration of Independence to say anything about slavery, it nevertheless remained a brilliant expression of Enlightenment ideals—ideals that still reverberate powerfully in the lives of Americans and other peoples today. "That all men are created equal; that they are endowed by their Creator with certain inalienable rights; that among these are life, liberty, and the pursuit of happiness"— these "truths" seemed "self-evident," even to eighteenth-century Americans divided by great distinctions of status and confronted with the glaring contradiction of black slavery. The Declaration of Independence set forth a philosophy of human rights that could be applied not only to Americans, but also to peoples everywhere. It was essential in giving the American Revolution a universal appeal.

AN ASYLUM FOR LIBERTY

It was a strange revolution that Americans had begun, one that on the face of it is not easily comprehended. A series of trade acts and tax levies do not seem to add up to a justification for independence. There was none of the legendary tyranny of history that had so often driven desperate peoples into rebellion. Yet by 1776 most Americans agreed with John Adams that they were "in the very midst of a Revolution, the most compleat, unexpected, and remarkable of any in the History of Nations." How then was it to be explained and justified?

Those Americans who looked back at what they had been

through could only marvel at the moderation and rationality of their Revolution. It was, said Edmund Randolph of Virginia, a revolution "without an immediate oppression, without a cause depending so much on hasty feeling as theoretic reasoning." Because the Americans, as Edmund Burke pointed out in one of his famous speeches in 1775, "augur misgovernment at a distance and snuff the approach of tyranny in every tainted breeze," they anticipated grievances even before they actually suffered them. Thus the American Revolution has always seemed to be an unusually intellectual and conservative affair—carried out not to create new liberties but to preserve old ones.

Throughout the imperial crisis American patriot leaders insisted that they were rebelling not against the principles of the English constitution, but on behalf of them. In order to express continuity with the great struggles for political liberty in England, they invoked historic English party designations and called themselves "Whigs," and branded the supporters of the crown "Tories." By emphasizing that it was the letter and spirit of the English constitution that justified their resistance, Americans could easily believe that they were simply protecting what Englishmen had valued from the beginning of their history.

Yet the colonists were mistaken in believing that they were struggling only to return to the essentials of the English constitution. The principles of the constitution that they defended were not those that were held by the English establishment in the mid eighteenth century. In fact, the Americans' principles were, as the Tories and royal officials tried to indicate, "revolution principles" outside the mainstream of English thought. Since the colonists seemed to be reading the same literature as other Englishmen, they were hardly aware that they were seeing the English tradition differently. Despite their breadth of reading and references, however, they concentrated on a set of ideas that ultimately gave them a peculiar conception of English life and an extraordinarily radical perspective on the English constitution they were so fervently defending.

The heritage of liberal thought that the colonists drew on was composed not simply of the political treatises of notable philosophers like John Locke but also of the writings of such eighteenth-century coffeehouse pamphleteers as John Trenchard and Thomas Gordon. Indeed, during the first half of the eighteenth century many of England's leading literary figures, such as Alexander Pope and Jonathan Swift, wrote out of a deep and bitter hostility to the great political, social, and economic changes they saw taking place around them. These critics thought that traditional values were being corrupted and that England was being threatened with ruin by the general commercialization of English life, as seen in the rise of such institutions as the Bank of England, powerful stock companies, stock markets, and the huge public debt. Believing that the crown was ultimately responsible for these changes, many of these writers championed a so-called "country" opposition to the deceit and luxury of the "court," which they associated with the crown and its networks of influence.

This country opposition had a long and complicated history in England. It stretched back at least to the early seventeenth century, to the Puritan opposition to the established church and the courts of the early Stuart kings, James I and Charles I. The English Civil War of the mid seventeenth century can in part be understood as an uprising of the local gentry, representing the counties or the "country" of England in the House of Commons, against the "court" surrounding the Church of England and the king. Such localist and grassroots opposition to far-removed central authorities was a recurring theme in English history as it would continue to be in American history.

In the eighteenth-century Anglo-American world, writers in this country-opposition tradition were especially fearful that executive power—particularly as it operated under the ministries of Sir Robert Walpole—was corrupting Parliament and English society in order to erect a fiscal-military state for the waging of war. Throughout the first half of the eighteenth century, these defenders of political liberty made ringing proposals to reduce and control what seemed to be the enormously expanded powers of the crown. Their goal was to recover the rights of the people and the original principles of the English constitution.

Many of the reforms they proposed were ahead of their time for England—reforms that advocated the right to vote for all adult males and not just the well-to-do property-holders, more liberty for the press, and greater freedom of religion. Other suggested reforms aimed at prohibiting salaried government "placemen" from sitting in the House of Commons, at reducing the public debt, and at obtaining such popular rights as equal representation for more people, the power to instruct members of Parliament, and shorter Parliaments. All these reform proposals combined into a widely shared conception of how political life in England should ideally be organized. In this ideal nation the parts of the constitution would be independent of one another, and members of Parliament would be independent of any "connection" or party. In other words, there would exist a political world in which no man would be beholden to another.

The Americans had long felt the relevance of these "country" ideas more keenly than the English themselves. These ideas had helped to explain the simple character of American life in contrast with the sophistication of England. But these opposition ideas had also justified the colonists' habitual antagonism to royal power. In the conflicts between the colonial assemblies and the royal governors in the first half of the eighteenth century, Americans had invoked these ideas off and on. Now, however, in the years after 1763, the need to explain the growing controversy with Britain gave this country-opposition ideology a new and comprehensive importance. It not only prepared the colonists intellectually for resistance, but also offered them a powerful justification of their many differences from what seemed to be a decayed and corrupted mother country.

These inherited ideas contained an elaborate set of rules for political action by the people. How were the people to identify a tyrant? How long should the people put up with abuses? How much force should they use? The answers to these questions came logically as events unfolded, and led the colonists almost irresistibly from resistance to rebellion. Step-by-step the colonists became convinced that the obnoxious efforts of crown officials to reform the empire were not simply the result of insensitivity to unique American conditions or mistakes of well-meant policy. Instead, Americans saw these as the intended consequences of a grand tyrannical design. In Thomas Jefferson's words the British reforms were nothing less than "a deliberate systematical plan of reducing us to slavery."

America, the colonists believed, was the primary object of this tyrannical conspiracy, but the goals of the conspiracy ranged far beyond the colonies. Americans were involved not simply in a defense of their own rights, but in a worldwide struggle for the salvation of liberty itself. When they looked over the past several centuries of European history, all they could see were the efforts of monarchs everywhere to build up state power in order to extract money from their subjects for the waging of war. By the late 1760s royal tyranny seemed to be gaining more ground, even in England itself. Americans earlier had read of the prosecution of the English radical John Wilkes for criticizing His Majesty's government in his *North Briton,* No. 45, and had made Wilkes and the number 45 part of their political symbolism. Then in 1768, Wilkes's four successive expulsions from a corrupt House of Commons, despite his repeated reelection by his constituents, marked for many Americans the twilight of representative government in Great Britain. Everywhere liberty appeared to be in retreat before the forces of tyranny. The struggles of "sons of liberty" in Ireland to win constitutional concessions were suppressed. The attempts of the freedom fighter Pascal Paoli and his followers to establish the independence of Corsica from France in the 1760s ended in failure. As Americans learned of these setbacks, they became convinced that America was the only place where a free popular press still existed and where the people could still elect representatives who spoke for them and them only.

By 1776 their picture of the immense struggle they were involved in was complete. And they could respond enthusiastically, as lovers of humanity and haters of tyranny, to the passionate appeal of Thomas Paine's *Common Sense* to stand forth for liberty:

> Every spot of the old world is overrun with oppression. Freedom hath been hunted round the globe. Asia and Africa have long expelled her. Europe regards her like a stranger, and England hath given her warning to depart. O! receive the fugitive, and prepare in time an asylum for mankind.

IV

CONSTITUTION-MAKING AND WAR

From the time royal authority had begun to disintegrate in 1774, Americans began thinking about creating new governments. They knew, as John Jay of New York declared, that they were "the first people whom heaven has favoured with an opportunity of deliberating upon and choosing forms of government under which they should live." And they aimed to make the most of this opportunity. During the summer of 1775, Samuel Adams and John Adams of Massachusetts, together with the Virginia delegation to the Continental Congress led by Richard Henry Lee, worked out a program for independence. They made plans to negotiate foreign alliances, to create a confederation or union for common purposes, and, most important, to establish new state governments.

THE STATE CONSTITUTIONS

The climax of their efforts came with the congressional resolutions of May 1776 advising the colonies to adopt new governments "under the authority of the people" and declaring "that the exercise of every kind of authority under the... Crown should be totally suppressed." Even before the Declaration of Independence the Congress had created a committee to form a confederation, and some of the states—New Hampshire, South Carolina, and Virginia—had begun working on new constitutions. With the May resolves and the Declaration of Independence, the other states also began to form new governments. By the end of 1776, New Jersey, Delaware, Pennsylvania, Maryland, and North Carolina had adopted new constitutions. Because they were corporate chartered colonies, Rhode Island and Connecticut were already republics in fact, and thus they simply confined themselves to eliminating all mention of royal authority in their charters. War conditions forced Georgia and New York to delay their constitution-making until 1777. Massachusetts had recovered its old charter, which the British had abolished in 1774, and was busy preparing to write a more permanent constitution.

In 1776–77, Americans concentrated much of their attention and energy on establishing these new state constitutions. The states, not the central government or Congress, were to test the Revolutionary hopes. In fact, forming new state governments, as Jefferson said in the spring of 1776, was "the whole object of the present controversy." For the aim of the Revolution had become not simply independence from British tyranny, but also the prevention of future tyrannies.

It was inevitable that Americans would draw up written documents. By the word *constitution* most eighteenth-century Englishmen meant not a written document, but the existing arrangement of government—that is, laws, customs, and institutions, together with the principles they embodied. Americans, however, had come to view a constitution in a different way. Ever since the seventeenth century they had repeatedly used their written colonial charters as defensive barriers against royal authority. During the imperial debate with Britain they had been compelled to recognize that laws made by Parliament were not necessarily constitutional or in accord with fundamental principles of rightness and justice. If the constitutional principles were to be protected from a powerful sovereign legislature, then somehow they had to be lifted out of the machinery of day-to-day government and set above it. The Americans' new state constitutions would therefore have to be fixed plans—single written documents, as the English constitution had never been—outlining the powers of government and specifying the rights of citizens.

As they wrote their new state constitutions, the Americans set about to institutionalize all that they had learned from their colonial experience and the recent struggle with England. Although they knew they would establish republics, they did not know precisely what forms the new governments should take. Their central aim was to prevent power, which they identified with the rulers or governors, from encroaching upon liberty, which they identified with the people or their representatives in the legislatures. Only this deep fear of gubernatorial or executive power can explain the radical changes Americans made in the authority of their now elected governors.

In their desire to root out tyranny once and for all, the members of the state conventions who drafted the new constitutions stripped the new elected governors of much of the power that the royal governors had exercised. No longer would governors have the authority to create electoral districts, control the meeting of the assemblies, veto legislation, grant lands, establish courts of law, issue charters of incorporation to towns, or, in some states, even pardon crimes. The Pennsylvania constitution, which was the most radical constitution of all the states, eliminated the governor outright. The constitution-makers surrounded all the new state governors with controlling councils whose members were elected by the assemblies. The weakened governors were to be elected annually (generally by the assemblies), limited in the times they could be reelected, and subject to impeachment.

However radical these changes in executive authority may have been, many Americans believed that they did not get to the heart of the matter and destroy the most insidious and dangerous source of despotism—the executive power of appointment to office. Since in a traditional monarchical society the distribution of offices, honors, and favors affected the social order, Americans were determined that their governors would never again have the capacity to dominate public life. The constitution-makers took exclusive control over appointments to executive and judicial offices from the traditional hands of the governors and gave it in large part to the legislatures. This change was justified by the principle of separation of powers, a doctrine Montesquieu had made famous in the mid eighteenth century. The idea behind maintaining the executive, legislative, and judicial parts of the government separate and distinct was not to protect each power from the others, but to keep the judiciary and especially the legislature free from executive manipulation—the very kind of manipulation that, Americans believed, had corrupted the English Parliament. Hence the new constitutions absolutely barred all executive officeholders and those receiving profits from the government from sitting in the legislatures. As a consequence, parliamentary cabinet government of the kind that existed in England was forever prohibited in America, and constitutional development moved off in a direction entirely independent of Great Britain—a direction that the American governments still follow.

Giving the powers that had been taken from the governors to the popular legislatures marked a radical shift in the responsibility of government. In English history the "government" had been identified exclusively with the crown or the executive. The representative body of Parliament had generally been confined to voting taxes, passing corrective legislation modifying the common law, and protecting the subjects' rights. But the new American state legislatures, in particular the popular lower houses of the assemblies, were no longer to be merely adjuncts of governmental power or checks on it. They were now given powers or prerogatives that formerly had belonged solely to the crown or chief magistrates, including making foreign alliances and granting pardons. This transferal of nearly all political authority to the people's representatives in the popular branch of the legislatures led some Americans, like Richard Henry Lee, to note that their new governments were "very much of a democratic kind," although "a Governor and a second branch of legislation are admitted." In 1776 many still thought of democracy as a technical term of political science that referred to rule by the people solely in the lower houses of the legislatures; the presence of aristocratic senates and monarchlike governors made the state constitutions not simple democracies but mixed governments like that of England with its king, House of Lords, and House of Commons—the last being the only representative and democratic part of the English constitution.

To ensure that the state legislatures fully embodied the people's will, the ideas and experience behind the Americans' view of representation were now drawn out and implemented. The Revolutionary state constitutions put a new emphasis on actual representation and the explicitness of consent. They did so by creating equal electoral districts, requiring annual elections, enlarging the suffrage, imposing residential requirements for both the electors and the elected, and granting constituents the right to instruct their representatives. The former attempts by the royal governors to resist extending representation to newly settled areas were now dramatically reversed. Towns and counties, particularly in the backcountry, were granted either new or additional representation in the state legislatures. Thus, Americans belatedly recognized the legitimacy of the western uprisings of the 1760s and '70s. Five states even stated that population ought to be the basis of representation, and wrote into their constitutions specific plans for periodic adjustments of their representation, so that, as the New York constitution of 1777 stated, it "shall for ever remain proportionate and adequate."

The confidence of the Revolutionaries in 1776 in their popular representative legislatures was remarkable. Except for disgruntled Tories and loyalists, few Americans expected these state legislatures to become tyrannical—in the Whig theory of politics it did not seem possible for the people to tyrannize over themselves. The idea, said John Adams in 1775, was illogical: "a democratic despotism is a contradiction in terms." Of course, the people were apt to be licentious or giddy; hence the republics needed not only governors but also upper houses in the legislature to counterbalance the popular lower houses of representatives. All the states except Pennsylvania, Georgia, and the new state of Vermont therefore provided for upper houses or senates, the designation taken from Roman history. The senators in these bicameral legislatures were to be republican versions of the English House of Lords—not representing any constituency in the society, but simply being the wisest and best, the natural aristocracy, in each state, who would revise and correct the well-intentioned but often careless measures of the people represented in the lower houses. Although the people in most of the states elected the senators, in 1776 the people were still thought to be represented exclusively in the lower houses of representatives just as the people of England were represented exclusively in their House of Commons. The process of election, in other words, was not yet considered to be the criterion of representation.

THE ARTICLES OF CONFEDERATION

At the same time that the Revolutionaries were creating their state constitutions, they were drafting a central government. Yet in marked contrast to the rich and exciting public explorations of political theory accompanying the formation of the state constitutions, there was little discussion of the plans for a central government. Whatever feelings of American nationalism existed in 1776, they paled before people's loyalties to their separate states. While the United States was new, most of the states had existed for a century or more and had developed symbols and traditions that were emotionally binding. When people in 1776 talked about their "country" or even their "nation," they usually meant Virginia or Massachusetts or Pennsylvania. Although the Declaration of Independence was drawn up by the Continental Congress, it was actually a declaration by "thirteen united States of America," who proclaimed that as "Free and Independent States, they have full

Power to levy War, conclude Peace, contract Alliances, establish Commerce, and to do all other Acts and Things which independent States may of right do." Despite all the talk of union, few Americans in 1776 could conceive of creating a single full-fledged continental republic.

Still, the Congress needed some legal basis for its authority. Like the various provincial conventions, it had been created in 1774 simply out of necessity, and it was exercising an extraordinary degree of political, military, and economic power over Americans. The Congress had established and maintained an army, issued a continental currency, erected a military code of law, defined crimes against the union, and negotiated abroad. With independence it was obvious to many leaders that a more permanent and legitimate union of the states was necessary. Although a draft of a confederation was ready for consideration by the Congress as early as mid-July 1776, not until November 1777, after heated controversy, did Congress present a document of union to the states for each of them to approve or reject. It took nearly four years, until March 1781, for all the states to accept this document and thereby legally establish the Articles of Confederation.

The Articles created a confederacy called the "United States of America" that was essentially a continuation of the Second Continental Congress. Congress was granted the authority earlier exercised by the British crown—to control diplomatic relations, requisition soldiers and money from the states, coin and borrow money, regulate Indian affairs, and settle disputes between the states. Although a simple majority of seven states was needed to settle minor matters, a larger majority, nine states, was required to resolve important issues, including engaging in war, making treaties, and coining and borrowing money. There was no real executive but only a series of congressional committees with a fluctuating membership.

The Union was stronger than many people expected. The

states were forbidden from conducting foreign affairs, making treaties, and declaring war. The citizens of each state were entitled to the privileges and immunities of the citizens of all states. All travel restrictions and discriminatory trade barriers between the states were eliminated. The judicial proceedings of each state were honored by all the states. These provisions, together with the substantial powers granted to the Congress, made the United States of America as strong as any similar republican confederation in history.

Nevertheless, the Americans' fears of distant central authority, intensified by a century of experience in the British Empire, left no doubt that this Confederation was something very different from a real national government. Under the Articles the crucial powers of commercial regulation and taxation—indeed all final lawmaking authority—remained with the states. Congressional resolutions continued to be, as they had been under the Continental Congress, only recommendations that the states were supposed to enforce. And should there be any doubts of the decentralized nature of the Confederation, Article 2 stated bluntly that "each State retains its sovereignty, freedom and independence, and every power, jurisdiction, and right, which is not by this confederation expressly delegated to the United States, in Congress assembled."

The "United States of America" thus possessed a literal meaning that is hard to appreciate today. The Confederation resembled more an alliance among closely cooperating sovereign states than a single government—something not all that different from the present-day European Union. Each state annually sent a delegation to the Confederation Congress (called by some states "our embassy"), and each delegation had only a single vote. The Confederation was intended to be and remained, as Article 3 declared, "a firm league of friendship" among states jealous of their individuality. Not only ratification of the Articles of Confederation, but also any subsequent changes in the document required the consent of all the states.

The local self-interest of the states prolonged the congressional debates over the adoption of the Articles and delayed their unanimous ratification until 1781. The major disputes— over representation, the apportionment of the states' contribution to the Union, and the disposition of the western lands—involved concrete state interests. Virginia and other populous states argued for proportional representation in the Congress, but these larger states had to give way to the small states' determination to maintain equal state representation in the unicameral Congress. After much wrangling over the basis for each state's financial contribution to the general treasury, the Confederation eventually settled on the proportion of people in each state, with slaves counting as three fifths of a person.

The states' rivalries were most evident in the long, drawn-out controversy over the disposition of the western lands between the Appalachian Mountains and the Mississippi River. The Articles sent to the states in 1778 for ratification gave the Congress no authority over the unsettled lands of the interior, and this omission delayed their approval. States like Virginia and Massachusetts with ancient charter claims to this western territory wanted to maintain control over the disposal of their land. But states without such claims, such as Maryland and Rhode Island, wanted the land pooled in a common national domain under the authority of Congress. Only in 1781 after Virginia, the state with charter rights to the largest amount of western territory, finally agreed to surrender its claims to the United States was the way prepared for other land cessions and for ratification of the Articles of Confederation by all the states. But the Confederation had to promise, in return for the cession of claims by Virginia and the other states, that the national domain would "be settled and formed into distinct republican states."

The Congress drew up land ordinances in 1784 and 1785 that provided for the Northwest Territory to be surveyed and formed into neat and orderly townships. In 1787 it adopted the famous Northwest Ordinance that at once acknowledged, as the British in the 1760s had not, the settlers' destiny in the West. In the succeeding decades the Land Ordinance of 1785 and the Ordinance of 1787 remained the basis for the sale and the political evolution of America's western territories.

Apart from winning the War of Independence, the Northwest Ordinance of 1787 was the greatest accomplishment of the Confederation Congress. It created an entirely new notion of empire and at a stroke solved the problem of relating colonial dependencies to the central authority that Great Britain had been unable to solve in the 1760s and '70s. When the monarchies of early modern Europe claimed new dominions by conquest or colonization, they inevitably considered these new provincial additions as permanently peripheral and inferior to the metropolitan center of the realm. But the Northwest Ordinance, which became the model for the development of much of the Southwest as well, promised an end to such permanent second-class colonies. It guaranteed to the settlers basic legal and political rights and set forth the unprecedented principle that new states settled in the West would enter the union "on an equal footing with the original States, in all respects whatsoever." Settlers could leave the older states with the assurances that they were not losing their political liberties and that they would be allowed eventually to form new republics as sovereign and independent as the other states of the Union. With such a principle there was presumably no limit to the westward expansion of the empire of the United States.

THE WAR FOR INDEPENDENCE

However important constitution-making of the states and the Union may have been to the Revolutionaries, it would mean nothing if independence were not achieved. Once Britain had determined to enforce its authority with troops, Americans knew that they had to take up arms to support their beliefs and their hopes for the future. For over a year before the Declaration of Independence, American and British forces had been at war. It was a war that would go on for nearly eight years—the longest conflict in American history until the Vietnam War two centuries later.

The war for independence passed through a series of distinct phases, growing and widening until what had begun in British eyes as a breakdown in governmental authority in a section of the empire became a worldwide struggle. For the first time in the eighteenth century, Great Britain found itself diplomatically isolated; at one point in 1779 it was even threatened with French invasion. The war for American independence thus eventually became an important episode in Britain's long struggle with France for global supremacy, a struggle that went back a century and would continue for another generation into the nineteenth century.

British troops had suffered heavy losses in their first clashes with the American militia in Massachusetts in the spring of 1775—at Lexington and Concord and especially in the bloody battle of Bunker Hill. This initial experience convinced the British government that it was not simply dealing with a New England mob, and it swept away almost every objection the members of the ministry had to a conquest of the colonies. During the summer of 1775 the Second Continental Congress appointed fourteen generals, authorized the invasion of Canada, and organized a Continental field army under George Washington. Aware that the southern colonies were suspicious of Massachusetts's fanaticism, John Adams pushed for the selection of the forty-three-year-old Virginia militia colonel as commander in chief. It was an inspired choice. Washington, who attended the Congress in uniform, looked the part: he was tall and composed, with a dignified soldier-like air that inspired confidence. He was, as one congressman said, "no harum-scarum, ranting, swearing fellow, but sober, steady, and calm."

All these congressional actions only confirmed the British government's realization that it was now involved in a military rather than a police action. This new understanding of what Britain was up against dictated a conventional eighteenth-century military policy of maneuver and battle between organized armies.

This change of strategy required that the British evacuate Boston and transfer their main forces to New York, with its presumably more sympathetic population, its superior port, and its central position. Accordingly, in the summer of 1776, Sir William Howe, who replaced Gage as commander in chief of the British army in North America, sailed into New York Harbor with a force of more than 30,000 men. Howe aimed to cut New England off from the other rebels and to defeat Washington's army in a decisive battle. He was to spend the next two frustrating years trying to realize this plan.

On the face of it, a military struggle seemed to promise all the advantage to Great Britain. Britain was the most powerful nation in the world, with a population of about 11 million, compared with only 2.5 million colonists, a fifth of whom were black slaves. The British navy was the largest in the world, with nearly half its ships initially committed to the American struggle. The British army was a well-trained professional force, numbering at one point in 1778 nearly 50,000 troops stationed in North America alone; and more than 30,000 hired German mercenaries were added to this force during the war.

To confront this military might the Americans had to start from scratch. The Continental Army they created numbered usually less than 5,000 troops, supplemented by state militia units of varying sizes. In most cases inexperienced amateur officers served as the American military leaders. Washington, the commander in chief, for example, had been only a regimental colonel on the Virginia frontier and had little first-hand knowledge of combat. He knew nothing about moving large masses of soldiers and had never conducted a siege of a fortified position. Many of Washington's officers were drawn from the middling ranks of the society and were hardly traditional gentlemen. There were innkeepers who were captains and shoemakers who were colonels, exclaimed an astonished French officer. Indeed, "it often happens that the Americans ask the French officers what their trade is in France." Not surprisingly, most British officers thought that the American army was "but a contemptible band of vagrants, deserters and thieves" and no match for His Majesty's redcoats. One British general even boasted that with a thousand grenadiers he could "go from one end of America to the other, and geld all the males, partly by force and partly by a little coaxing."

Yet such a contrast of numbers and abilities was deceptive, for the British disadvantages were immense and perhaps overwhelming—even at the beginning when their opportunities to put down the rebellion were greatest. Great Britain had to carry on the war three thousand miles across the Atlantic, with consequent problems of communications and logistics; even supplying the army with food became a problem. At the same time, Britain had to wage a different kind of war from any the country had ever fought in the eighteenth century. A well-trained army might have been able to conquer the American forces, but, as one French officer observed at the end, America itself was unconquerable. The great breadth of territory and the wild nature of the terrain made conventional maneuverings and operations difficult and cumbersome. The fragmented and local character of authority in America inhibited decisive action by the British. There was no nerve center anywhere whose capture would destroy the rebellion. The British generals came to see that engaging Washington's army in battle ought to be their main objective; but, said the British commander in chief, they did not know how to do it, "as the enemy moves with so much more celerity than we possibly can."

Washington for his part realized at the outset that the American side of the war should be defensive. "We should on all occasions avoid a general Action," he told Congress in September 1776, "or put anything to the risque unless compelled by a necessity into which we ought never to be drawn." Although he never saw himself as a guerrilla leader and concentrated throughout on creating a professional army with which he was often eager to confront the British in open battle, his troops actually spent a good deal of time skirmishing with the enemy, harassing them and depriving them of food and supplies whenever possible. In such circumstances the Americans' reliance on amateur militia forces and the weakness of their organized army made the Americans, as a Swiss officer noted, more dangerous than "if they had a regular army." The British never clearly understood what they were up against—a revolutionary struggle involving widespread support in the population. Hence they continually underestimated the staying power of the rebels and overestimated the strength of the loyalists. And in the end, independence came to mean more to the Americans than reconquest did to the English.

From the outset the English objective could never be as simple and clear-cut as the Americans' desire for independence. Conquest by itself could not restore political relations and imperial harmony. Many people in England were reluctant to engage in a civil war, and several officers actually refused on grounds of conscience to serve in America. Although the king, the bulk of the Parliament, and most members of the English ministry were intent on subjugating America by force, the British commanders appointed in 1775 never shared this overriding urge for outright coercion. These commanders—Sir William Howe and his brother Admiral Richard, Lord Howe, who was in charge of the navy—saw themselves not simply as conquerors but also as peacemakers. They had in fact been authorized by Lord North to seek a political solution while putting down the rebellion with force. Consequently they interrupted their military operations with peace feelers to Washington and the Continental Congress, and they tried to avoid plundering and ravaging the American countryside and ports out of fear of destroying a hope for reconciliation. This "sentimental manner of waging war," as Lord George Germain, head of the American Department, called it, weakened the morale of British officers and troops and left the loyalists confused and disillusioned.

The policy of the Howe brothers was not as ineffectual initially as it later appeared. After defeating Washington on Long Island in August 1776 and driving him from New York City in the fall of 1776, General Howe had Washington in pell-mell retreat southward. Instead of pursuing Washington across the Delaware River, Howe resorted to a piecemeal occupation of New Jersey. He extended his lines and deployed brigade garrisons at a half-dozen towns around the area with the aim of gradually convincing the rebels that the British army was invincible. Loyalist militiamen emerged from hiding and through a series of ferocious local struggles with patriot groups began to assume control of northern New Jersey. Nearly 5,000 Americans, including one signer of the Declaration of Independence, came forward to accept Howe's offer of pardon and to swear loyalty to the crown. American prospects at the end of 1776 were as low as they ever would be during the war. These were, as Thomas Paine wrote, "times that try men's souls."

The Howes' policy of leniency and pacification, however, was marred by plundering by British troops and by loyalist recriminations against the rebels. But even more important in undermining the British successes of 1776 were Washington's brilliant strokes in picking off two of Howe's extended outposts at Trenton on December 25–26, 1776, and at Princeton on January 3, 1777. With these victories Washington forced the British to withdraw from the banks of the Delaware and to leave the newly formed bands of loyalists to fend for themselves. Patriot morale soared, oaths of loyalty to the king declined, and patriot militia moved back into control of local areas vacated by the withdrawing British troops. With New Jersey torn by ferocious partisan or guerrilla warfare, the British again had to reconsider their plans.

The British strategy for 1777 involved sending an army of 8,000, including 3,000 Germans and several hundred Indians, under General John Burgoyne southward from Canada by way of Lake Champlain to recapture Fort Ticonderoga. Near Albany, Burgoyne was to join a secondary force under Lieutenant Colonel Barry St. Leger, moving eastward through the Mohawk Valley, and General Howe, advancing northward from New York City through the Hudson Valley. The ultimate aim of the campaign was to isolate New England and break the back of the rebellion. It was assumed in Britain that General Howe would cooperate with Burgoyne. But Howe continued to believe that there was widespread loyalist support in the middle states and decided to capture Philadelphia, the seat of the congressional government. Howe moved on Philadelphia by sea and landed after much delay at the head of Chesapeake Bay in late August 1777. Believing he could not give up the Continental capital without a struggle, Washington confronted Howe at Brandywine, Pennsylvania, on September 11 and later on October 4 at Germantown and was defeated in both battles. But his defeats were not disastrous: They proved that the American army was capable of organized combat, and they prevented Howe from moving north to help Burgoyne. Howe's capture of Philadelphia demonstrated that loyalist sentiment reached only as far as British arms, and it scarcely justified what happened to Burgoyne's army in the North.

After St. Leger's force was turned back at Oriskany, New

York, in the summer of 1777, Burgoyne and his huge, slow-moving entourage from Canada increasingly found their supply lines stretched thin and their flanks harassed by patriot militia from New England. Burgoyne's baggage train was over three miles long; his personal baggage alone took up over thirty carts. By felling trees, destroying bridges, and diverting streams, the patriots did all they could to make the wild terrain even more impassable than it was. Burgoyne had to build over forty new bridges as well as repair old ones. At one point he was covering less than one mile a day. This sluggish pace only worsened the problem of supply. One of his lieutenants declared that for every hour Burgoyne spent thinking how to fight his army he had to devote twenty hours figuring out how to feed it.

While Burgoyne's slow advance gave the American forces in the Hudson Valley needed time to collect themselves, the British army was diminishing. When 900 of Burgoyne's men attempted to seize provisions from a patriot arsenal in Bennington, Vermont, they were defeated by 2,000 New England militia under John Stark. Another 900 redcoats were detached to garrison Ticonderoga. Believing that his reputation rested on the success of his Canadian invasion, Burgoyne determined to press on. On September 13–14 he crossed the Hudson, cutting off his supply lines and communications with his rear. When he reached Saratoga, he confronted a growing American force of over 10,000 men under General Horatio Gates. Two bloody battles, in which General Benedict Arnold distinguished himself, convinced Burgoyne of the hopelessness of his situation, and in October 1777 he surrendered his entire army to the Americans.

Saratoga was the turning point. It suggested that reconquest of America might be beyond British strength. It brought France openly into the struggle. And it led to a change in the British command and a fundamental alteration in strategy.

From the beginning of the rebellion France had been secretly supplying the Americans money and arms in the hope of revenging its defeat in the Seven Years' War. In 1776, Benjamin Franklin had gone to Paris to serve as the unofficial American ambassador. By 1777, French ports had been opened to American privateers, and French officers were joining Washington's army. It seemed only a matter of time before France recognized the new republic. The British ministry realized at once the significance of Burgoyne's surrender, and by appointing the Carlisle Commission early in 1778 made new efforts to negotiate a settlement. The British government now offered the rebels a return to the imperial status before 1763—indeed, everything the Americans had originally wanted. These British overtures, which Franklin skillfully used in Paris to play on French fears of an Anglo-American reconciliation, led the government of King Louis XVI in February 1778 to sign two treaties with the United States: one a commercial arrangement, the other a military alliance pledged to American independence—the first and only military alliance for the United States until that of NATO in 1949. In 1779 Spain became allied with France, in the hope of recovering its earlier losses from England, especially Gibraltar. And in 1780 Russia formed a League of Armed Neutrality, which nearly all of the maritime states of Europe eventually joined. For the first time in the eighteenth century, Britain was diplomatically isolated.

After 1778 putting down the rebellion became secondary to Britain's global struggle with the Bourbon powers, France and Spain. The center of the war effort in America shifted seaward and southward as Britain sought to protect its possessions in the West Indies. General Howe was replaced by Sir Henry Clinton; a more ruthless policy was adopted, including the bombardment of American ports, raids on the countryside, and attempts to buy off the rebel leaders, with Benedict Arnold's treason being the most conspicuous result. Arnold was a brilliant battlefield commander who came to resent the way state and congressional officials were treating him. In 1779 he entered into secret negotiations with Sir Henry Clinton to turn over West Point to the British in return for money and a royal commission in the British army. Although the plot to turn over West Point was thwarted in 1780, Arnold escaped and became a British general. For successive generations of Americans, Arnold personified the meaning of treason.

As part of their new strategy the British intended to abandon Philadelphia and assume a defensive position in New York and Rhode Island. Concentrating their forces in the West Indies, they aimed to secure military control of ports in the Deep South, restore civil royal government with loyalist support, and then methodically move the army northward as a screen behind which local loyalists would gradually pacify the rebel territories. This strategy was based on an assumption that the South, with its scattered, presumably more loyalist population living in fear of Indian raids and slave uprisings, was especially vulnerable to the reassertion of British authority.

The British evacuation of Philadelphia in June 1778 offered Washington an opportunity to attack the extended slow-moving British column. Although Washington's troops had suffered terribly from lack of food and clothing during the previous winter of 1777–78 at Valley Forge, they had actually emerged a more unified and disciplined fighting force. Led by Baron von Steuben, a former aide-de-camp to the king of Prussia, the army trained and drilled and reorganized itself and developed a new pride and esprit. Despite opposition from some of his generals, especially General Charles Lee, who had no confidence in von Steuben's training, Washington was eager to test his newly disciplined troops against Clinton's withdrawing redcoats. Although the hard-fought battle of Monmouth, New Jersey, on June 28 ended in a draw, Washington and Congress considered it a victory, for the American regulars had stood up to the best of the British regulars.

Washington's ultimate success as the American commander in chief, however, never stemmed from his military abilities. He was never a traditional military hero. He had no smashing, stunning victories, and his tactical and strategic maneuvers were never the sort that awed men. Instead, it was his character and political talent and judgment that mattered most. His stoicism, dignity, and perseverance in the face of seemingly impossible odds came to symbolize the entire Revolutionary cause. As the war went on year after year, his stature only grew, and by 1779 Americans were celebrating his birthday as well as the Fourth of July. Washington always deferred to civilian leadership and never lost the support of the Congress, even when exaggerated rumors of a cabal involving Thomas Conway, an Irish-born French officer, and General Horatio Gates, the victor at Saratoga, seemed to threaten his position in the fall and winter of 1777–78. He was always loyal to his fellow officers in the Continental Army and they to him; they trusted him, and with good reason. What he lacked in military skill he made up with prudence and wisdom. When in the wake of the French alliance the French nobleman the Marquis de Lafayette, who had been in the struggle since 1777, proposed a Franco-American scheme for conquering Canada, the excited Congress readily agreed. Washington, however, pointed out that France had her own interests and was scarcely to be trusted in the retaking of Canada, and the scheme quietly died.

With the center of British operations removed to the South, Washington was left in the North over the next few years trying to put down mutinies in his army and pleading for French military and naval support. All he could do was avoid giving Clinton an opportunity to defeat him in a decisive battle and watch in frustration at the initial successes of the new British strategy of pacification in the South. During the winter of 1778–79 the British captured Savannah and Augusta and restored royal civil government in Georgia. Although constant American militia attacks slowed the British advance, on May 12, 1780, with the surrender of General Benjamin Lincoln and his American army of 5,500, the British finally took Charleston, South Carolina. It was the greatest American loss of soldiers in the entire war. A new, hastily assembled American southern army under General Gates rashly moved into South Carolina to stop the British offensive. On August 16, 1780, at Camden, South Carolina, Gates suffered a devastating defeat, which destroyed not only his new American army but his military reputation as well. But the British were not able to consolidate their gains and give the loyalists the military protection needed to pacify the countryside. Loyalist retaliations against Whig patriots for past harsh treatment, along with British plunder of the backcountry, particularly by the ruthless commander Colonel Banastre Tarleton, drove countless Georgians and Carolinians into partisan activity in support of the Revolution. Colorful leaders like Thomas Sumter and Francis Marion organized irregular bands of patriots to harass the loyalists and the British army. The war in the lower South became a series of bloody guerrilla skirmishes with atrocities on both sides.

In the South, Lord Cornwallis was now in command of the British forces. He was impatient with the gradual policy of pacification and was eager to demonstrate British strength by dramatically carrying the war into North Carolina. With his army constantly bedeviled by patriot guerrillas, he had just begun moving northward when he learned that his left flank had been destroyed at King's Mountain on October 7, 1780. The news forced him to return to South Carolina. In the meantime the Americans had begun organizing a third southern army under the command of a thirty-eight-year-old ex-Quaker from Rhode Island, Nathanael Greene, recently quartermaster general of the Continental Army. Shrewdly avoiding a direct confrontation with Cornwallis, Greene compelled the British to divide their forces. On January 17,

1781, at Cowpens in western South Carolina, a detached corps of Greene's army under Daniel Morgan defeated "Bloody" Tarleton's Tory Legion and changed the course of British strategy in the South.

Cornwallis cut his ties with his base in Charleston and turned his army into a mobile striking force, determined to chase down the elusive American army. After an indecisive battle with Greene at Guilford Courthouse on March 15, 1781, Cornwallis's tired and battered soldiers withdrew to Wilmington on the North Carolina coast with the intention of moving the seat of war northward into Virginia. Thus ended the British experiment with a thorough program of pacification. During the spring and summer of 1781, patriot forces regained control of most of the lower South.

Although marauding by British forces in the summer of 1781 frightened Virginians and humiliated Governor Thomas Jefferson, Cornwallis could not convince his commander in chief, Clinton, in New York to make Virginia the center of British military operations. The haggling between the two generals enabled the Americans to bolster their Virginia troops under the command of Lafayette. Cornwallis's withdrawal to the Virginia coast and his eventual isolation at Yorktown gave the combined American and French army of nearly 17,000 men under Washington and the Comte de Rochambeau the opportunity it was looking for. The French fleet under Admiral de Grasse moved into Chesapeake Bay and blocked Cornwallis's planned escape by sea. Thus surrounded and bombarded at Yorktown, Cornwallis was forced to surrender his army of 8,000 troops to Washington in October 1781. Britain's policy since 1778 of spreading its control along the entire Atlantic seaboard depended on maintaining naval superiority; and when this superiority was temporarily lost in 1781, the entire plan collapsed. Although the war dragged on for several months, everyone knew that Yorktown meant American independence.

The long war was costly for the new country: more than

25,000 American military deaths—nearly 1 percent of the population, second only to the Civil War in deaths relative to population.

Despite the end of the war, the peace still had to be won. The main objective of the new nation—independence from Great Britain—was clear and straightforward. But this objective and others concerning America's territorial boundaries and its rights to the Newfoundland fisheries had to be reconciled with the aims of America's ally, France, and with the aims of France's ally, Spain, which had been at war with Great Britain since 1779. The United States and France had pledged in 1778 not to make a separate peace with Britain. But since France was bound to Spain against Britain until Gibraltar was recovered, there was great danger of American interests getting lost in the machinations of the European powers. Despite the desire of France and Spain to humiliate Britain, neither Bourbon monarchy really wanted a strong and independent American republic. Spain in particular feared the spread of republicanism among its South American colonies and sought to protect its interests in the Mississippi Valley.

Although Franklin, John Adams, and John Jay, the American negotiators in Europe, were only, in Adams's words, "militia diplomats," they wound their way through the intricate corridors of international politics with professional diplomatic skill. Despite instructions from the Congress to do nothing without consulting the French, the American diplomats decided to negotiate with Britain alone. By hinting at the possibility of weakening the Franco-American alliance, they persuaded Great Britain to recognize the independence of the United States and to agree to much more generous boundaries for the new country than the French and particularly the Spanish were willing to support. On the west, the United States reached to the Mississippi River; on the south, to the thirty-first parallel; and on the north, to roughly the present boundary with Canada. The American negotiators then presented this preliminary Anglo-American treaty to

France and persuaded the French to accept it by suggesting that allies must conceal their differences from their enemies. The prospect of American peace with Britain now compelled Spain to abandon its demands for Gibraltar and to settle for the return of East and West Florida. In the final treaty signed on September 3, 1783, the United States, by shrewdly playing off the mutual fears of the European powers, gained both independence and concessions that stunned the French and indeed all of Europe. It was the greatest achievement in the history of American diplomacy.

V

REPUBLICANISM

A military victory over Great Britain may have been essential for the success of the Revolution, but for Americans it was scarcely the whole of the Revolution. Although the Revolution had begun as a political crisis within the empire, by 1776 it was no longer merely a colonial rebellion. From 1775, when independence and hence the formation of new governments became imminent, and continuing throughout the war, nearly every piece of writing about the future was filled with extraordinarily visionary hopes for the transformation of America. But not just America's government and society would be transformed; its role in the world would be changed as well. Americans had come to believe that the Revolution promised nothing less than a massive reordering of their lives—a reordering summed up in the conception of republicanism.

THE NEED FOR VIRTUE

This republicanism was in every way a radical ideology—as radical for the eighteenth century as Marxism was to be for the nineteenth century. It meant more than simply eliminating a king and establishing an elective system of government. It added a moral and idealistic dimension to the political separation from England—a dimension that promised a fundamental shift in values and a change in the very character of American society.

Republicanism intensified the radicalism of the "country" ideology that Americans had borrowed from opposition groups in English society, and linked it with the older and deeper European currents of thought that went back to antiquity. These classical currents of thought—essentially explanations for the decline of the ancient Roman Republic—set forth republican ideals and values—about the good life, citizenship, political health, and social morality—that have had a powerful and lasting effect on Western culture.

These classical ideas had been revived by Renaissance writers, particularly Machiavelli, and had been carried into seventeenth-century English thought by such writers as James Harrington, the poet John Milton, and Algernon Sidney. It was under the influence of these classical republican ideas that England in the seventeenth century had executed its king, Charles I, and had tried its brief experiment in republicanism, the Commonwealth (1649–53). By the eighteenth century these classical republican ideals had spread throughout western Europe and had become a kind of counterculture for many dissatisfied Europeans. In countless writings and translations, ranging from Charles Rollin's popular histories of antiquity to Thomas Gordon's translations of Tacitus and Sallust, eighteenth-century European and British intellectuals evoked the utopian image of an earlier Roman republican world of simple farmer-citizens enjoying liberty and arcadian virtue. Reformers everywhere saw this idealized ancient world as an alternative to the sprawling monarchies, with their hierarchies, luxury, and corruption, that they had come to despise in their own time.

In the excitement of the Revolutionary movement, these classical republican values came together with the long-existing European image of Americans as a simple, egalitarian, liberty-loving people to form one of the most coherent and powerful ideologies the Western world had yet seen. Many of the ambiguities Americans had felt about the rustic provincial character of their society were now clarified. What some had seen as the crudities and deficiencies of American life could now be viewed as advantages for republican government. Independent American farmers who owned their own land no longer had to be regarded as primitive folk living on the edges of European civilization and in the backwaters of history. Instead, they could now be seen as equal citizens naturally equipped to realize the republican values intellectuals had espoused for centuries.

Inevitably, the new American states in 1776 became republics. Everyone knew that these new republics with their elective systems had not only political but also moral and social significance. Republicanism struck directly at the ties of blood, kinship, and dependency that lay at the heart of a monarchical society. In a monarchy individuals were joined together as in a family by their common allegiance to the king. Since the king, in the words of the English jurist William Blackstone, was the "pater familias of the nation," to be a subject was in fact to be a kind of child—weak and dependent, sinful and lacking in self-restraint. Yet monarchies, based on the presumption that human beings were corrupt, had persisted almost everywhere for centuries because they offered security and order. Left alone and free, people, it was assumed, would run amuck, each doing what was right in his own eyes. Such a selfish people had to be held together from above, by the power of kings who created trains of dependencies and inequalities, supported by standing armies, strong religious establishments, and a dazzling array of titles, rituals, and ceremonies.

Republicanism challenged all these assumptions and practices of monarchy. By throwing off monarchy and becoming republicans in 1776, Americans offered a different conception of what people were like and new ways of organizing both the state and the society. The Revolutionary leaders were not naïve and they were not utopians—indeed, some of them had grave doubts about the capacities of ordinary people. But by adopting republican governments in 1776 all of them necessarily held to a more magnanimous conception of human nature than did supporters of monarchy.

Republics demanded far more morally from their citizens than monarchies did of their subjects. Republics lacked all the accouterments of patronage and power possessed by monarchies. If republics were to have order, it would have to come from below, from the people themselves, from their consent and their virtue, that is, from their willingness to surrender their personal desires to the public good. Much of the Revolutionary rhetoric was filled with exhortations to the people to act virtuously, telling them, as Samuel Adams did, that "a Citizen owes everything to the Commonwealth." Republicanism thus stressed a morality of social cohesion and devotion to the common welfare, or *res publica*. Several of the states in 1776—Massachusetts, Pennsylvania, and Virginia—even adopted the name "commonwealth" to express better their identification with the seventeenth-century English revolutionaries and their new dedication to the public good.

Republican citizens, in short, had to be patriots. Patriots were not simply those who loved their country but those who were free of dependent connections. As Jefferson wrote in his *Notes on the State of Virginia,* "dependence begets subservience and venality, suffocates the germ of virtue, and prepares fit tools for the designs of ambition." Hence the sturdy independent yeomen, Jefferson's "chosen people of God," were regarded as the most incorruptible and the best citizens for a republic. The celebration of the independent farmer in the years following the Revolution was not a literary conceit but an imperative of republican government.

The individual ownership of property, especially landed property, was essential for a republic, both as a source of independence and as evidence of a permanent attachment to the community. Those who were propertyless and dependent—young men and women—could thus be justifiably denied the vote because, as a convention of Essex County, Massachusetts, declared in 1778, they were "so situated as to have no wills of their own." In Europe, dependency was common because only a few possessed property. But, as one Carolinian wrote in 1777, "the people of America are a people of property; almost every man is a freeholder." Jefferson was so keen on this point that he proposed in 1776 that the new commonwealth of Virginia guarantee at least fifty acres of land for every citizen.

These republican communities of independent citizens presented an inspiring ideal. But history had shown that republics were an especially fragile kind of state, highly susceptible to faction and internal disorder. Because republics were so utterly dependent on the virtue of the people, theorists like Montesquieu concluded that they had to be small in territory and homogeneous in character. The only existing European republican models—the Netherlands, and the Italian and Swiss city-states—were small and compact, not fit models for the sprawling new nation of the United States. According to the best political science of the day, when a large country with many diverse interests attempted to establish a republic, as England had tried in the seventeenth century, the experiment was sure to end in some sort of dictatorship like that of Oliver Cromwell.

It is not surprising therefore that Americans in 1776 embarked on their experiment in republicanism in a spirit of risk and high adventure. Yet most American Revolutionaries were enthusiastic and remarkably confident of success. They believed that they were naturally virtuous and thus ideally suited for republican government. Were not the remarkable displays of popular order in the face of disintegrating royal governments in 1774–75 evidence of the willingness of the American people to obey their governments without coercion? Did they not possess the same hardy character the ancient republican citizens had? In contrast to England, where most people were tenants or landless workers, most Americans, at least most white adult males, owned their own land. Americans told themselves that they were a young and vigorous people, not yet dissipated by the aristocratic luxuries and indolent pleasures of the Old World.

THE RISING GLORY OF AMERICA

The exhilaration Americans felt in 1776 came not simply from their belief that they were in the vanguard of a world-wide republican revolution that would eventually topple decrepit monarchies everywhere. They also believed that they were destined to bring about a new flowering in the arts and sciences; they would become the leaders of the international "republic of letters." Many American intellectuals came to believe that the torch of civilization was being passed across the Atlantic to the New World, where it would burn even more brightly. Despite their rejection of the luxury and corruption of the Old World, the American Revolutionaries never meant to repudiate the best of English and European culture, but rather to embrace and fulfill it. "The enterprising genius of the people," declared an excited Joel Barlow, "promises a most rapid improvement in all the arts that embellish human nature."

In light of their former colonial status and their earlier widespread expressions of cultural inferiority, their presumption of becoming the cultural leaders of the Western world is jarring, to say the least. Yet the evidence is overwhelming that Revolutionary leaders and artists imagined America eventually becoming the place where the best of all the arts and sciences would flourish. When the Revolutionaries talked of "treading upon the ground of Greece and Rome" they meant not only that they would erect republican governments, but also that they would in time have their own Homers and Virgils—in the words of historian David Ramsay, their own "poets, orators, criticks, and historians equal to the most celebrated of the ancient commonwealths of Greece and Italy."

Such dreams, bombastic as they seem in retrospect, were grounded in the best scholarly thinking of the day and had helped to give Americans the confidence to undertake their

Revolution. They knew, as philosopher David Hume had pointed out, that free states bred learning among the populace, and a learned populace was the best source of genius and artistic talent. But they knew as well that the arts and sciences were inevitably moving westward. From mid-century on, they had read and extolled Bishop Berkeley's "Verses on the Prospect of Planting Arts and Learning in America," which set forth the conventional notion of a western cycle of empire from the Middle East to Greece, from Greece to Rome, from Rome to western Europe, and from western Europe across the Atlantic to the New World. As early as 1759, an unsympathetic British traveler noted that the colonists were "looking forward with eager and impatient expectation to that destined moment when America is to give the law to the rest of the world." So common became this theme of the transit of civilization westward that it led to the creation of a new literary genre, "The Rising Glory of America" poem, which, it seems, every gentleman with literary aspirations tried his hand at.

Of course, not every American intellectual was sure of the New World's ability to receive the inherited torch of Western culture, and some doubted whether America's primitive tastes could ever sustain the fine arts. But many of the Revolutionary leaders envisioned America's becoming not only a libertarian refuge from the world's tyranny, but also a worthy place where, in the words of Ezra Stiles, the enlightened president of Yale, "all the arts may be transported from Europe and Asia and flourish with ... an augmented lustre."

If Americans were to exceed Europe in dignity, grandeur, and taste, they would somehow have to create a republican art that avoided the Old World vices of overrefinement and luxury. The solution lay in the taut rationality of republican classicism, which allowed artistic expression without fostering corruption and social decay. It emphasized, as the commissioners who were charged with supervising the construction of public buildings in Washington, D.C., put it in

1793, "a grandeur of conception, a Republican simplicity, and that true elegance of proportion, which correspond to a tempered freedom excluding Frivolity, the food of little minds."

Such a neoclassical art was not an original art in any modern sense, but it was never intended to be. The Americans' aim, in their literature, painting, and architecture, was never to break irreparably from English forms but to give new and fresh republican spirit to old forms, to isolate and exhibit in their art the external and universal principles of reason and nature. Poets in the wilds of the New York frontier thus saw nothing incongruous in invoking comparisons with Virgil or Horace. The Connecticut poet John Trumbull was compared to Swift. Milton, Dryden, and Pope were all adopted without embarrassment as models for imitation. Even Noah Webster, despite all his experiments with developing a peculiar American language, never intended that the elegant style of Addison should be abandoned.

The criterion of art in this neoclassical era lay not in the genius of the artist or in the novelty of the work, but rather in the effect of the art on the audience or spectator. Consequently, someone like Joel Barlow could believe that his long epic poem *The Vision of Columbus* (1787), precisely because of its high moral and republican message, could excel in grandeur even Homer's *Iliad*. And the painter John Trumbull, not to be confused with his cousin the poet, could conclude that the profession of painting was not trivial and socially useless as long as the artist depicted great events and elevated the spirit of the viewer. Washington, as much as he loved the theater, could only justify it on the grounds that it would "advance the interest of private and public virtue" and "polish the manners and habits of society." There was nothing startling about Thomas Jefferson's choice of the Maison Carrée, a Roman temple at Nîmes from the first century A.D., as a model for the new republican state capitol to be built along the mud-lined streets of a backwoods town in Virginia. Since architecture to Jefferson was "an art which shows so much," it was particularly important for the new nation that appropriate inspirational forms be adopted, even though a Roman temple was hard to heat and acoustically impossible.

The cultural relics of these neoclassical dreams are with Americans still: not only in the endless proliferation of Greek and Roman temples, but in the names of towns like Syracuse and Troy; in the designation of political institutions like the capitols and the senates; in political symbols like the goddess Liberty and numerous Latin mottoes; and in the poetry and songs, such as "Hail Columbia." But the spirit that once inspired these things, the meaning they had for the Revolutionaries, has been lost and was being lost even as they were being created. How many Americans today know what the pyramid and eye on the Great Seal mean, even though the device appears on every dollar bill? Who today reads Joel Barlow's epic poetry or Timothy Dwight's *Conquest of Canaan?* Much of the art of the 1790s, except for portraits, was neglected and scorned by subsequent generations. All of these neoclassical dreams were soon overwhelmed by the egalitarian democracy that resulted from the Americans' grand experiment in republicanism.

EQUALITY

The community of the arts and science was called "the republic of letters" because the participants in that community— writers, painters, scientists, and other creative people—were not there by hereditary right: They necessarily had to be talented. Who, it was asked, remembered the fathers or sons of Homer and Euclid? Artistic talent, declared Thomas Paine, was not hereditary. In a republic individuals were no longer destined to be what their fathers were. Ability, not birth or whom one knew, was what mattered. "In monarchies," declared David Ramsay of South Carolina, "favor is the source of preferment; but, in our new forms of government, no one can command the suffrages of the people, unless by his superior merit and capacity." This, said Ramsay, was what Americans meant by equality—the very "life and soul" of republicanism.

Equality—the most powerful idea in all of American history—predicted an end to the incessant squabbling over position and rank and the bitter contentions of factional politics that had afflicted the colonial past. Since this discord was thought to be rooted in the artificial inequalities of colonial society, created and nourished largely through the influence and patronage of the British crown, the adoption of republicanism promised a new era of social harmony.

But republican equality did not mean the elimination of all distinctions. Republics would still have an aristocracy, said Jefferson, but it would be a natural, not an artificial one. The republican leaders would resemble not the luxury-loving money-mongering lackeys of British officialdom but the stoical and disinterested heroes of antiquity—men, like George Washington, who seemed to Americans to embody perfectly the classical ideal of a republican leader.

Yet in the end, equality meant more than careers open to the talented few. The Revolutionaries' stress on the ability of common people to elect those who had integrity and merit presumed a certain moral capacity in the populace as a whole. Good republicans had to believe in the common sense of the common people. Ordinary people may not have been as educated or as wise as gentlemen who had college degrees, but they were more trustworthy. They were frank, honest, and sincere, qualities that were essential for republican government. Republican America would end the deceit and dissembling so characteristic of courtiers and monarchies. "Let those flatter who fear," said Jefferson in 1774; "it is not an American art."

But republicanism went even further in promoting equality.

The most enlightened eighteenth-century thinking challenged the scornful manner in which for centuries the aristocratic few had viewed the common many. In our egalitarian-minded age it is difficult for us to appreciate the degree of contempt with which for centuries the aristocracy and gentry of traditional monarchical societies had regarded the lower orders. Common people, when they were noticed at all, were often looked upon as little better than animals. Even some of the Revolutionary leaders were not beyond an occasional disparaging remark about ordinary folk. George Washington once called the common people "the grazing multitude," Alexander Hamilton spoke of the "unthinking populace," and early in his career John Adams, who never forgot he had once been one of them, referred to ordinary folk as the "common Herd of Mankind."

Other Americans too did not hesitate to qualify their belief in the natural equality of mankind. Many balked at even including Indians or blacks within the sphere of men; and when most men thought about women in these terms, it was only to emphasize women's difference from men, not their equality. Some continued to believe that God had ordained permanent distinctions between the saved and the damned. Still others, while admitting that all men had the same senses of sight, hearing, smell, taste, and touch, argued that men of genius, the elite, had developed their senses to the point where they had become more sensitive than common people.

Although this distinction based on different degrees of sensibility helped to justify the continued separation of gentlemen from commoners, ultimately the eighteenth century's emphasis on the senses and sensibility opened the way to a greater belief in the equality of people. If human beings were separated from one another not by innate characteristics but by learned ones, learned by the environment operating through the senses, then everyone at least began life with the same blank slate.

Jefferson's affirmation in the Declaration of Independence that all men are created equal was, as he later recalled, simply "the common sense" of the age. By the latter part of the eighteenth century, to be enlightened was to believe in the natural equality of all men. Even those as aristocratic as William Byrd and Governor Francis Fauquier of Virginia conceded that all men, even men of different nations and races, were born equal and that "the principal difference between one people and another proceeds only from the differing opportunities of improvement." "White, Red, or Black; polished or unpolished," declared Governor Fauquier in 1760; "Men are Men." That only education and cultivation separated one man from another was the most explosive idea of the eighteenth century, indeed, of all modern thinking.

By placing a radically new value on knowledge acquired through the senses rather than through reason, John Locke's *Essay Concerning Human Understanding* (1690) had given a new significance to the capacities of ordinary people. Perhaps only a few were capable of reason and intellectual achievement, but all people were capable of receiving impressions through their senses.

Thus, despite the patrician sense of gentlemanly distinctiveness expressed by the Revolutionary leaders—a frank and unabashed commitment to elitism that profoundly separates them from us today—what in the end remains remarkable is the degree to which they accepted the equality of all people. A common nature linked people together in natural affection and made it possible for them to be friends and to share each other's moral feelings. There was something in each human being—some sort of moral sense or sympathetic instinct— that bound everyone together in a common humanity and made possible natural compassion and morality. Jefferson expressed great doubts about the intellectual abilities of blacks, but he conceded that in their moral sense they were the equal of whites. It was obvious that reason was unequally distributed in people, but all persons, however humble and however uncultivated, had in their hearts a moral intuition that told them right from wrong. Indeed, some believed that educated gentlemen had no greater sense of right and wrong than plain unlettered people.

Jefferson believed that differences between people were created by experience, by the environment operating through people's senses. But Jefferson and other enlightened eighteenth-century thinkers realized the dangers of pure sensationalism. How could men and women control the environment's chaotic bombardment of their senses? Something was needed to structure their turbulent and jumbled experiences. Otherwise, human personalities, said the Scottish-born lawyer of Pennsylvania James Wilson, quoting David Hume, would become "a bundle or collection of different perceptions, which succeed each other with an inconceivable rapidity...in a perpetual flux and movement." A society composed only of fluctuating sensations was impossible; something had to tie people together intuitively and naturally. As Jefferson said, "the Creator would indeed have been a bungling artist, had he intended man for a social animal, without planting in him social dispositions." Jefferson and other American leaders thus modified their stark Lockean environmentalism by positing this natural social disposition, a moral instinct, a sense of sympathy, in each human being. Such a moral gyroscope— identified with Scottish moral or commonsense thinking and resembling Kant's categories—was needed to counteract the worst and most frightening implications of Lockean sensationalism and to keep individuals level and sociable in a confused and chaotic world.

These beliefs in the natural affection, moral sense, and benevolence of people were no utopian fantasies but the enlightened conclusions of the eighteenth-century science of society. While most clergymen continued to urge Christian love and charity upon their parishioners, many other educated and enlightened people sought to secularize Christian love and find in human nature itself a scientific imperative for loving one's neighbor as oneself. There seemed to be a natural principle of attraction that pulled people together, a moral principle that was no different from the principles that operated in the physical world. "Just as the regular motions and harmony of the heavenly bodies depend upon their mutual gravitation towards each other," said the Massachusetts preacher Jonathan Mayhew, so too did love and benevolence among people preserve "order and harmony" in the society. Love between humans was the gravity of the moral world, and it could be studied and perhaps even manipulated more easily than the gravity of the physical world. Enlightened thinkers like the Earl of Shaftesbury and Adam Smith thus sought to discover these hidden forces that moved and held people together in the moral world. They looked for forces in the social world that could match the great eighteenth-century scientific discoveries of the hidden forces—gravity, magnetism, electricity, and energy—that operated in the physical world. Thinkers like John Witherspoon, president of Princeton, dreamed of a time "when men, treating moral philosophy as Newton and his successors have done natural philosophy, may arrive at greater precision." Out of such dreams was modern social science born.

Of course, many intellectuals in the eighteenth century still believed that republican society could be held together only by the kind of ancient masculine and martial virtue expressed, for example, in Jacques-Louis David's classical republican painting, *The Oath of the Horatii,* exhibited in Paris in 1786. But many others had come to believe that the kind of classical republican virtue represented in David's painting was too demanding and too severe for the enlightened, polite, and civilized societies of the eighteenth-century Atlantic world.

For many enlightened thinkers, people's natural instinct to be sociable and benevolent became a modern substitute for the ascetic classical virtue of the ancient world. Virtue became less the harsh and martial self-sacrifice of antiquity and more the modern willingness to get along with others for the sake of peace and prosperity. Mingling in drawing rooms, clubs, coffeehouses, and even commercial exchanges—partaking of the innumerable daily comings and goings of modern life—created friendship and sympathy that helped to hold society together. This modern virtue was more Addisonian than Spartan and was capable of being expressed by women as well as men; some said that women were even more capable than men of sociability and benevolence.

The Revolutionary leaders, of course, had varying degrees of confidence in people's natural sympathy and benevolence. While someone like Alexander Hamilton soon came to doubt people's moral capacities, others like Thomas Paine and Thomas Jefferson remained very optimistic; indeed, they thought that the natural harmony of society might even replace much of governmental authority itself. If only the natural tendencies of people to love and care for one another were allowed to flow freely, unclogged by the artificial interference of government, particularly monarchical government, the most optimistic republicans believed that society would prosper and hold itself together.

Unlike liberals of the twenty-first century, the most liberal-minded of the eighteenth century tended to see society as beneficent and government as malevolent. Social honors, social distinctions, perquisites of office, business contracts, legal privileges and monopolies, even excessive property and wealth of various sorts—indeed, all social inequities and deprivations—seemed to flow from connections to government, in the end from connections to monarchical government. "Society," said Paine in a brilliant summary of this liberal view, "is produced by our wants and government by our wickedness." Society "promotes our happiness *positively* by uniting our affections," government "*negatively* by restraining our vices." Society "encourages intercourse," government "creates distinctions." The emerging liberal Jeffersonian view that the least government was the best was based on just such a hopeful belief in the natural harmony of society.

This liberal belief in the capacity of affection and benevolence to hold republican societies together may have been as unrealistic and as contrary to human nature as the traditional belief in austere classical virtue. Certainly hard-nosed skeptics like Alexander Hamilton came to doubt its efficacy. But for a moment in the enthusiasm of revolution, many Americans imagined a new and better world emerging, a world, they said, of "greater perfection and happiness than mankind has yet seen."

A NEW WORLD ORDER

In that new and better world that many Revolutionary leaders envisioned, war itself might be abolished. Just as liberal Americans in their Revolutionary state constitutions sought a new kind of domestic politics that would end tyranny, so too did many of them seek a new kind of international politics that would promote peace among nations. This emphasis alone gave the American Revolution worldwide significance.

Throughout the eighteenth century, liberal intellectuals had looked forward to a new enlightened world in which corrupt monarchical diplomacy, secret alliances, dynastic rivalries, and balances of power would be abolished. Since war was promoted by the dynastic ambitions, the bloated bureaucracies, and the standing armies of monarchies, then the elimination of monarchy would mean the elimination of war itself. A world of republican states would encourage a peace-loving diplomacy—one based on the natural concert of international commerce. If the people of the various nations were left alone to exchange goods freely among themselves—without the corrupting interference of selfish monarchical courts, irrational dynastic rivalries, and the secret double-dealing diplomacy of the past—then, it was hoped, international politics would become republicanized and pacified.

Suddenly in 1776, with the United States isolated and outside Europe's mercantile empires, the Americans had both an opportunity and a need to put into practice these liberal ideas about international relations and the free exchange of goods. Thus commercial interest and Revolutionary idealism blended to form the basis for much American thinking about foreign affairs that lasted well into the twentieth century; to some extent this blending is still present in American thinking about the world.

"Our plan is commerce," Thomas Paine told Americans in 1776, "and that, well attended to, will secure us the peace and friendship of all Europe; because it is the interest of all Europe to have America a free port." America had no need to form traditional military alliances. Trade between peoples alone would be enough. Indeed, for Paine and other liberals peaceful trade among the people of the various nations became the counterpart in the international sphere to the sociability of people in the domestic sphere. Just as enlightened thinkers like Paine and Jefferson foresaw a republican society held together solely by the natural affection of people, so too did they envision a world held together by the natural interests of peoples in commerce. In both the national and international spheres monarchy and its intrusive institutions and monopolistic ways were what prevented a natural harmony of people's feelings and interests.

In 1776 members of the Continental Congress attempted to embody these liberal principles in a model treaty that would be applied to France and eventually to other nations. This model treaty, drafted mainly by John Adams in July 1776, promised the greatest possible commercial freedom and equality between nations. Were the principles of the model treaty "once really established and honestly observed," John Adams later recalled, "it would put an end forever to all maritime war, and render all military navies useless." In duties and trade restrictions foreigners were to be treated as one's own nationals were treated. Even in wartime trade was to be kept flowing. Neutral nations were to have the right to trade with and carry the goods of the belligerent nations— the right expressed in the phrase "free ships make free goods." The list of contraband articles—that is, articles subject to seizure by belligerents, including those articles owned by neutral nations—were to be limited and would not include, for example, provisions and naval stores. In addition, blockades of belligerent ports had to be backed up by naval power and not simply declared on paper.

Ultimately the Americans did not get much of what they wanted in the treaties they signed with France in 1778. Although the commercial treaty they made with France did contain the principles of free trade, they also had to agree to a traditional political and military alliance. Despite this concession to realpolitik, however, the Americans' enlightened dream of a new world order based on commerce was not lost. In 1784 the United States authorized a diplomatic commission composed of Jefferson, Adams, and Franklin to negotiate commercial treaties with sixteen European states based on the liberal principles of a revised 1784 model treaty. The hope was to have America lead the way to an "object so valuable to mankind as the total emancipation of commerce and the bringing together all nations for a free intercommunication of happiness."

The major European nations, however, refused to open themselves freely to American trade; and only two states— Prussia and Sweden, peripheral powers with little overseas trade—agreed to sign liberal treaties with the United States. Yet despite the indifference of most European states, many Americans, and especially Thomas Jefferson and James Madison, remained confident of the power of commerce to influence international politics. This confidence in the power of American commerce and these liberal principles of free trade continued to influence many Americans' thinking about the world into the early decades of the nineteenth century. It explains the idealistic efforts of the Jeffersonian Republicans to resort to nonimportation measures and eventually in 1807 to a wholesale embargo of American overseas trade as a grand experiment in what Jefferson called "peaceful coercion." Indeed, even today the common resort to economic sanctions in place of military force is a legacy of these enlightened principles.

VI

REPUBLICAN

SOCIETY

The republican Revolution had transforming effects every-where. It shook up traditional hierarchies, cut people loose from their customary ties as never before, and brought authority of all sorts into question. To be sure, there was no immediate collapse of the social order, and no abrupt and wholesale destruction of familiar social institutions. But everywhere there were alterations in the way people related to government, to the economy, and to one another. Many of these changes were the accelerations of deeply rooted forces long in motion. But others were the recent and direct results of the Revolution itself.

EFFECTS OF THE WAR

One sudden effect of the Revolution was the departure of tens of thousands of loyalists—or Tories, as the patriots called them. The loyalists may have numbered close to half a million, or 20 percent of white Americans. Nearly 20,000 of them fought for the crown in regiments of His Majesty's army, and thousands of others served in local loyalist militia bodies. As many as 60,000 to 80,000 loyalists, it is estimated, left America for Canada and Great Britain during the Revo-lution, although many of these returned after the war and were reintegrated into American society. Although the loyal-ists came from all ranks and occupations of the society, a large proportion of them belonged to the upper political and social levels. Many had been officeholders and overseas merchants involved with government contracting; in the North, most were Anglicans. Their regional distribution was likewise un-even. The loyalists were a tiny minority in New England and Virginia; but in western frontier areas, where hostility to east-ern oppression went back to pre-Revolutionary times, they were numerous. The loyalists also made up a considerable part of the population in the regions of New York, New Jersey, Pennsylvania, and the Deep South, where the British army offered them protection. Their flight, displacement, and retirements created a vacuum at the top that was rapidly filled by patriots. The effects were widespread. Crown and Tory property and lands valued at millions of pounds were confiscated by the Revolutionary governments and almost immediately thrown onto the market. The resulting speculation contributed to the sudden rise and fall of fortunes during the Revolutionary years.

The South suffered the greatest disruptions from the war. Not only did it lose its established markets for its tobacco and other staple crops, but the British freed tens of thousands of its slaves to fight for the crown. At the end of the war the British settled these former slaves in Canada, the West Indies, and other parts of the world. Indeed, the British army was perhaps the greatest single instrument of emancipation in America until the Civil War. But these dislocations only speeded up an agricultural diversification that had begun before the Revolution. The Upper South in particular recovered rapidly. Tobacco production in the 1780s equaled prewar levels, involving, however, many new participants and new marketing arrangements.

Although the war had devastating effects on particular sections and individuals, its overall results were stimulating. Merchants who had previously been on the fringes of economic activity found new opportunities at the center of things. In Massachusetts, provincial families like the Higginsons, Cabots, and Lowells quickly moved into Boston to form the basis for a new Massachusetts elite. By the end of the war many, like Governor James Bowdoin of Massachusetts, could "scarcely see any other than new faces," a change, he said, almost as "remarkable as the revolution itself." The same mobility was duplicated less notably but no less importantly elsewhere. New merchants pushed out in all directions in search of new markets, not only into the once restricted colonial areas of the West Indies and South America, but throughout Europe and even as far away as China.

Postwar trade with Great Britain quickly reached its earlier levels. By the 1780s, aggregate figures suggest an amazing recovery of commerce. Yet gross statistics do not do justice to the extent of change that was involved. In all the states there were new sources of supply, new commercial patterns, and new and increased numbers of participants in the market. The wartime collapse of British imports had encouraged domestic manufacturing; and although the purchase of British goods resumed with the return of peace, societies were formed to promote protective legislation for American manufacturing. Although exports abroad soon surpassed their prewar levels, they now represented a smaller part of America's total economic activity. Already people were beginning to turn inward—toward trading with one another instead of abroad; a remarkable spread of internal commerce would soon generate demands for new roads and canals. In these changing circumstances, towns without hinterlands to exploit began a relative decline. A city like Newport, Rhode Island, had been a flourishing colonial port; but lacking an inland area for supply and marketing, it now rapidly slipped into commercial insignificance.

The Revolutionary War itself was at once both a disruptive and a creative force, and it touched nearly everyone one way or another. Like all wars, it destroyed familiar channels of trade and produced new sources of wealth. During the eight long years of the war, perhaps as many as 200,000 men bore arms at one time or another in the Continental Army and state militias. All these soldiers had to be clothed, fed, housed, armed, and moved about. Thomas Paine did not realize the half of it when he wrote in 1776 that "the necessities of an army create a new trade." The inexhaustible needs of three armies—the British and French as well as the American—for everything from blankets and wagons to meat and rum brought into being hosts of new manufacturing and entrepreneurial interests and made market farmers out of husbandmen who before had scarcely ever traded out of their neighborhoods. At the same time military purchasing agents became the breeding grounds for both petty entrepreneurs and powerful postwar capitalists like Robert Morris of Pennsylvania and Jeremiah Wadsworth of Connecticut, who were in charge of congressional financing and contracting.

Because the Revolutionary states were reluctant to tax their citizens, and because the Congress did not have the legal authority to tax, the American governments had to rely on borrowing to pay for all the goods they needed for the war effort. But borrowing could scarcely raise the needed sums. Both the Congress and the state governments therefore resorted to the extensive printing of paper currency. These bills of credit, which the governments promised to redeem at some future date, were given to citizens in return for supplies and services.

The currency that was issued by the congressional and state governments eventually totaled nearly $400 million in paper value and led to a socially disintegrating inflation. By 1781, $167 of congressional paper was worth only $1 in specie (gold and silver), and the depreciation of the states' bills was nearly as bad. While creditors, wage-earners, and those on relatively fixed incomes were hurt by this inflation, many of those who were most active in the economy—those who were buying and selling goods rapidly—were able to profit. These circulating government bills enabled countless commodity farmers and traders to break out of a simple barter or personal-book-account economy and to specialize and participate more independently and impersonally in the market than they had in the past. In the end, the Revolution released latent economic energies that set America on a course of rapid commercial development rarely matched by any country in the history of the world.

EFFECTS OF THE REVOLUTION

Beyond these immediate social and economic effects of the war, there were other, deeper, and more long-lasting forces that were greatly affected by the Revolution and its republican ideas. Despite a slackening of immigration and the loss of the loyalist émigrés, the population continued to grow. In fact, the 1780s saw the fastest rate of demographic growth of any decade in American history—a consequence of early marriages and high expectations for the future. After being delayed for several years in the late 1770s by intermittent warfare against the British and Indians, this swelling population resumed its roll westward. "The population of the country of Kentucky will amaze you," wrote one migrant in 1785; "in June, 1779, the whole number of inhabitants amounted to 176 only, and they now exceed 30,000." Within a decade Kentucky had become more populous than most of the colonies had been at the time of the Revolution. In fact, more western territory was occupied in the first post-Revolutionary generation than in the entire colonial period.

Of course, the dreams of white Americans for this trans-Appalachian West had little or no place for the tens of thousands of Indians who lived there. Although the Confederation Congress in 1787 promised that "the utmost good faith shall always be observed towards the Indians, [and that] their lands and property shall never be taken from them without their consent," the Northwest Ordinance itself took for granted that the destiny of the Northwest belonged to the white American settlers.

Although many whites admired the Indians for their freedom, the Anglo-American idea of liberty and independence was very different from that of the Indians. Where ordinary white American men conceived of freedom in terms of owning their own plot of cultivated agricultural land, Indian males saw liberty in terms of their ability to roam and hunt at will. Like many American gentry, the Indian warriors did not believe they should actually work tilling fields; they thus left manual labor to the women—to the shock of many whites. Indeed, so unnatural to European Americans was the idea of women farming that they had a hard time acknowledging that the Indians practiced any agriculture at all. Ultimately, this denial that the Indians actually cultivated the land became the white Americans' justification for taking it from them. They expected the Indians to become farmers, that is, to become civilized, or to get out of the way of the settlers.

The achievement of American independence from Great Britain in 1783 was a disaster for the Indians. Many of the tribes in the Northwest and Southwest had allied with the British, and with the peace treaty they discovered that Great Britain had ceded sovereignty over their land to the United States. As one speaker from the Weas complained to their British ally upon learning of the treaty, "In endeavouring to assist you, it seems we have wrought our own ruin." Because so many of the Indians had fought on the side of the British, Americans tended to regard as enemies even those Indians who had been their allies during the Revolution. By the 1780s many western Americans shared the expectation of the Indian fighter George Rogers Clark that all the Indians would eventually be wiped out.

Based as it was on an unequal and hierarchical society, the British crown could easily treat the Indians as subjects. But the new Republic of the United States did not have subjects, only equal citizens. Since white Americans could scarcely conceive of the Indians as citizens equal to themselves, they had to regard the Indian peoples as foreign nations. In the 1780s the Confederation government sought to assume control of Indian affairs and to establish peaceful relations with the Indians. Although the Confederation Congress repeatedly spoke of its desire to be just and fair with the Indians, it considered them as conquered nations. In several treaties between the Confederation government and some of the various nations or tribes in the mid-1780s, the United States attempted to establish more or less fixed boundary lines between whites and Indians in return for Indian cessions of rights to land. Believing that America owned the lands by right of conquest, the United States offered the Indians no compensation for the ceded lands.

But the Confederation government was weak. Not only did the states ignore the Confederation's treaties and make their own agreements with the Indians, but white settlers and squatters acted without regard to any authority. The assumption of the congressional land ordinances of the 1780s that people would move west in a neat and orderly fashion was illusory. Instead, people shunned the high-priced land, violated Indian treaty rights, and moved irregularly, chaotically, and unevenly, jumping from place to place and leaving huge chunks of unsettled land and pockets of hemmed-in Indians behind them. By 1787 many of the Indians had repudiated the treaties some of their members had been compelled to sign and attempted to form loose confederations in order to resist the white advance. War and bloodshed inevitably followed.

Despite the presence of the Indians, the American population continued to grow and move in a spectacular manner, further weakening the traditional forms of social organization. Such a mobile population, one Kentuckian told Madison in 1792, "must make a very different mass from one which is composed of men born and raised on the same spot.... They see none about them to whom or to whose families they have been accustomed to think themselves inferior." The ideology of republicanism intensified these developments. In a republic, declared a writer in 1787 in the *American Museum* (the

most important of the several new American magazines created in the postwar years), "the idea of equality breathes
through the whole and every individual feels ambitious, to be
in a situation not inferior to his neighbour."

This republican equality now became a rallying cry for
people in the aspiring middling ranks who were now more
openly resentful than before of those who had presumed to
be their social superiors. The widespread protest against the
Society of the Cincinnati expressed this resentment. In 1783,
Revolutionary army officers, in order to commemorate and
perpetuate their participation in the Revolutionary War,
formed the hereditary Order of the Cincinnati, named after
the legendary Roman republican leader Cincinnatus, who
had retired from war to take up his plow. Although Washington had agreed to lead the organization, the Cincinnati
aroused angry hostility. Old patriots such as Samuel Adams
thought that the Order represented "as rapid a Stride towards
an hereditary Military Nobility as was ever made in so short
a time." This sort of ferocious criticism forced the army officers to deny some of their pretensions and the Cincinnati
soon became just another one of the many pressure groups
emerging in a country that, as the governor of South Carolina
said in 1784, had gone "society mad."

Some fervent equality-minded citizens attacked distinctions of all kinds, including belonging to private social clubs
and wearing imported finery. Gentlemen in some areas of the
North found that the traditional marks of social authority—
breeding, education, good manners—were becoming liabili-
ties for political leadership. Ordinary citizens now claimed
the right to the titles—*Mr.* and *Mrs.*—that had once belonged
only to the gentry. In this new republican society no one
wanted to be dependent on anyone else. In Philadelphia the
proportion of white servants in the workforce, which at mid-
century had constituted 40 to 50 percent, now declined
precipitously; and by the end of the century indentured
servitude had virtually disappeared. Foreign visitors were

stunned by the unwillingness of American servants to address their masters and mistresses as superiors and by the servants' refusal to admit that they were anything but "help." For many Americans, living in a free country meant never having to tip one's cap to anyone.

This growing egalitarianism did not mean that wealth was distributed more evenly in post-Revolutionary America. On the contrary: Wealth was far more unequally distributed after the Revolution than it had been before. Nevertheless, Americans felt more equal, and that was what mattered. After all, wealth as a means by which one person claimed superiority over another was more easily accepted than birth, breeding, family heritage, gentility, or even education, and it was the one most easily matched or overcome by exertion. Relationships were now more and more based on money rather than social position. Towns, for example, stopped assigning seats in their churches by age and status and began auctioning the pews off to the highest bidders. Wealthy men began to brag of their humble origins—something not commonly done before. When a South Carolina politician in 1784 was praised in the press for being a self-established man who "had no relations or friends, but what his money made for him," a subtle but radical revolution in thinking had taken place. When Benjamin Franklin's autobiography was posthumously published in the 1790s, the nineteenth-century celebration of the "self-made man" was born.

By the end of the eighteenth century the paternalism of the former monarchical society was in disarray. Apprentices were no longer dependents in the master's family; rather, they became trainees within a business that was more and more conducted outside the household. Artisans did less "bespoke" or "order" work for particular patrons on whom they were personally dependent; instead, they increasingly produced for impersonal markets. Masters in the various crafts, instead of being patriarchs paternalistically tied to their journeymen, became employers paying their employees cash wages.

As masters turned into employers and journeymen into employees, their interests became more distinct and conflicting than they had been before. In 1786 for the first time in American history, employees participated in a strike against their employers. In response, masters now resorted to the courts to enforce what had once been seen as a mutual and personal relationship.

REPUBLICAN REFORMS

Since the Revolutionaries believed that people were not born to be what they might become, they were confident that they had the ability, like no people in modern times, to remake themselves and the future as they saw fit. Dr. Benjamin Rush was very excited by the enthusiasm shown by Americans at a fete held in Philadelphia in July 1782 in honor of the birth of the heir to the French crown. He realized that Protestant Americans were now eagerly celebrating what they had been long taught to hate—the French Catholic monarchy. The fete, he said, "shows us in the clearest point of view that there are no prejudices so strong, no opinions so sacred, and no contradictions so palpable, that will not yield to the love of liberty." Since free and republican America was "in a plastic state," where "everything is new & yielding," it "seems destined by heaven," said Rush, "to exhibit to the world the perfection which the mind of man is capable of receiving from the combined operation of liberty, learning, and the gospel upon it."

Americans in the years following their Revolution set about reforming their culture, in their strenuous efforts to bring their ideas and manners into accord with their new republican governments. Enlightened men could believe, as Samuel Stanhope Smith, soon to be president of Princeton, told James Madison shortly after independence, that new habitual principles, "the constant authoritative guardians of virtue," could be created and nurtured by republican laws, and these principles, together with the power of the mind, could give people's "ideas and motives a new direction." By the repeated exertion of reason—by "recalling the lost images of virtue: contemplating them, and using them as motives of action, till they overcome those of vice again and again ... until after repeated struggles, and many foils, they at length acquire the habitual superiority"—by such exertions it seemed possible for Americans to create a society of "habitual virtue." From these premises flowed the Revolutionaries' efforts at moral and social reformation, much of their republican iconography, and, perhaps most important, the republicans' devotion, in Smith's words, to "the great importance of an early virtuous education."

Americans knew that tyranny was founded on ignorance. As the Massachusetts constitution of 1780 stated, "Wisdom and knowledge, as well as virtue diffused generally among the people ... [are] necessary for the preservation of their rights and liberties." The consequence of this Revolutionary thinking was a torrent of speeches and writings on the importance of education that has rarely been matched in American history. America's national obsession with education was born with the Revolution.

Although by 1776 there were only nine colleges in America, sixteen more were founded in the next twenty-five years. At the same time, many Revolutionary leaders drew up elaborate plans for establishing comprehensive publicly supported school systems. Although little immediately came of these plans, the republican ideal of the state's fundamental responsibility to educate all of its citizens remained alive and was eventually realized in the common school movement of the early nineteenth century.

Formal schooling, of course, was only a part of what the Revolutionaries meant by education. Americans formed numerous scientific organizations and medical societies and flooded the country with all sorts of printed matter. Three quarters of all the books and pamphlets published in America between 1637 and 1800 appeared in the final thirty-five years of the eighteenth century. Between 1786 and 1795 twenty-eight learned and gentlemanly magazines were established, six more in these few years than in the entire colonial period. Since Americans sought to become a civilized and genteel people, they wanted advice manuals for everything—from how to write letters to friends to how to rise on one's toes before a curtsy. Two thirds of all the American spelling books published in the eighteenth century were issued in the final seventeen years of the century between 1783 and 1800. By the early nineteenth century Noah Webster's comprehensive speller, first published in 1783, had sold 3 million copies.

Although writing and spelling were important, they were not as important as reading. The few private libraries that had existed in the large cities in the colonial period were now supplemented by publicly supported libraries, which in turn sponsored increasing numbers of reading clubs, lectures, and debating societies. Although newspapers were relatively rare prior to the Revolution, they were soon being created at astonishing rates, which soon made the American people the greatest newspaper-reading public in the world.

Because Americans thought of themselves as peculiarly a people of sentiment and sensibility, they were eager to create charitable and humanitarian societies. Indeed, there were more such humanitarian societies formed in the decade following the Revolution than were created in the entire colonial period. These charitable societies treated the sick, aided the industrious poor, housed orphans, fed imprisoned debtors, built huts for shipwrecked sailors, and, in the case of the Massachusetts Humane Society, even attempted to resuscitate those suffering from "suspended animation," that is, those such as drowning victims who appeared to be dead but actually were not.

Jefferson and other Revolutionary leaders drew up plans for liberalizing the harsh penal codes inherited from the colonial period. Pennsylvania led the way by abolishing the death penalty for all crimes except murder. Instead of, as in the past, publicly punishing criminals by such bodily penalties as whipping, mutilation, and execution, Pennsylvania began the experiment of confining criminals in solitary cells in penitentiaries that were designed to be schools of reformation. Other states soon followed with these new kinds of prisons. Nowhere else in the Western world were such penal reforms carried as far as they were in America.

Schools, benevolent associations, and penitentiaries—all these were important for reforming the society and making it more republican. But none of them could compare in significance with that most basic social institution, the family. By rejecting monarchy and the older paternalistic ties of government and asserting the rights and liberties of individuals, the Revolution inevitably affected relationships within the family. It abolished the older English patterns of inheritance and the aristocratic legal devices that had sought to maintain the stem line of the estate (entail) and to sacrifice the interests of younger children to the eldest son (primogeniture). Many of the states passed new inheritance laws that recognized greater equality among sons and daughters. Everywhere novelists and others writing in the post-Revolutionary years stressed the importance of raising children to become rational and independent citizens.

Although there was little legal change in the authority of husbands over their wives, the traditional relationship was now questioned in ways that it had not been earlier. The Revolution made Americans conscious of the claim for the equal rights of women as never before. Some women now objected to the word "obey" in the marriage vows because it turned the woman into her husband's "slave." Under pressure, even some of the older patriarchal laws began to change. The new republican states now recognized women's rights to divorce and to make contracts and do business in the absence of their husbands. Women began asserting that rights belonged not just to men, and that if women had rights, they could no longer be thought of as inferior to men. In 1790, Judith Sargent Murray, daughter of a prominent Massachusetts political figure, writing under the pseudonym "Constantia," published an essay, "On the Equality of the Sexes." Popular writings everywhere now set forth models of a perfect republican marriage. It was one based on love, not property, and on reason and mutual respect. And it was one in which wives had a major role in inculcating virtue in their husbands and children. These newly enhanced roles for wives and mothers now meant that women ought to be educated as well as men. Consequently during the two decades following the Revolution, numerous academies were founded solely for the advanced instruction of females, a development unmatched in other parts of the world. Even though women were almost everywhere denied the right to vote, some of the upper strata of women began to act as political agents in their own right, using their social skills and various unofficial social institutions to make connections, arrange deals, and help create a ruling class in America.

ANTISLAVERY

No institution was more directly affected by the liberalizing spirit of the Revolution than chattel slavery. To be sure, the enslavement of nearly half a million blacks was not eradicated at the Revolution, and in modern eyes this failure amid all the high-blown talk of liberty and equality becomes the one glaring and even hypocritical inconsistency of the Revolutionary era. Indeed, far more blacks lived in slavery at the end of the Revolutionary era than at the beginning, and slavery in parts of America, far from declining, was on the verge of its greatest expansion. Nevertheless, the Revolution had a powerful effect in eventually bringing an end to slavery in America. It suddenly and effectively ended the social and intellectual environment that had allowed slavery to exist everywhere for thousands of years without substantial questioning.

The colonists had generally taken slavery for granted as part of the natural order of a monarchical society and as one aspect of the general brutality and cheapness of life in those premodern and prehumanitarian times. Originally, slavery had been regarded merely as the most base and degraded status in a hierarchy of many statuses and ranks of freedom and unfreedom, and that attitude had lingered on. Bondage and servitude in many forms had continued to exist in pre-Revolutionary America, and the colonists had felt little need to defend slavery any more than other forms of debasement. Now, however, republican citizenship suddenly brought into question all kinds of personal dependency. For the first time in their history Americans were compelled to confront the slavery in their midst as an aberration, as a "peculiar institution," and, if they were to retain it, to explain and justify it.

Even before the Declaration of Independence, the libertarian atmosphere of the imperial controversy had exposed the excruciating contradiction of slavery. James Otis in 1764 had declared that all the colonists were "by the law of nature freeborn, as indeed all men are, white or black.... Does it follow that 'tis right to enslave a man because he is black?" How could white Americans contend for liberty while holding other men in slavery? As the crisis deepened, such questions became more and more insistent.

The initial efforts to end the contradiction were directed at the slave trade. In 1774, the Continental Congress urged abolishing the slave trade, which a half-dozen northern states quickly did. In 1775 the Quakers of Philadelphia formed the first antislavery society in the world, and soon similar societies were organized elsewhere, even in the South. During the war Congress and the northern states together with Maryland gave freedom to black slaves who enlisted in their armies. In various ways the Revolution worked to weaken the institution.

In the North, slavery of a less harsh sort than existed in the South had been widespread but not deeply rooted in the society or economy. Slavery in the North was thus susceptible to political pressure in a way that was not true in the South, and it very slowly and haltingly began to recede. In the decades following the Revolution the northern states moved to destroy the institution, and by 1804 every northern state had committed itself to emancipation in one form or another. In many cases blacks themselves took the lead in using the Revolutionary language of liberty to attack slavery. By 1810 the number of free blacks in the northern states had grown from several hundred in 1770 to nearly 50,000. The Revolutionary vision of a society of independent freeholders led Congress in the 1780s specifically to forbid slavery in the newly organized Northwest Territory between the Appalachians and the Mississippi. The new federal Constitution promised, in 1808, an end to the international importation of slaves, which many hoped would cripple the institution. In fact, all of the Revolutionary leaders, including southerners like Jefferson, Patrick Henry, and Henry Laurens, deplored the injustice of slavery and assumed that it would soon die away. This was perhaps the most illusory of the several illusions the Revolutionary leaders had about the future of America.

At first, it seemed that slavery might be eliminated even in the South. More antislavery societies existed in the South than in the North, and manumissions became very frequent in the immediate post-Revolutionary period; in Virginia alone the number of free blacks increased from 3,000 in 1780 to 13,000 by 1790. But in the end, slavery in the South was too entrenched to be legislatively or judicially abolished. Southern whites who had been in the vanguard of the Revolutionary movement and among the most fervent spokesmen for its libertarianism now began developing a self-conscious sense of difference from the rest of America that they had never had to the same degree before. By the 1790s the South was living with a growing fear, fed by the Negro insurrections in Santo Domingo, of the newly invigorated American presumption that people everywhere, white or black, yearned for freedom.

REPUBLICAN RELIGION

In the New World that Americans were building—a republican world of "comprehensive benevolence" expressing "every divine and social virtue"—religion had an important role to play. After all, delivering America from sin and luxury was precisely what republicanism called for. Thus, unlike the church in Europe, American churches perceived no threat from revolution or republicanism. Except for the Anglicans, Protestant ministers were in the forefront of the Revolutionary movement. In fact, it was the clergy who made the Revolution meaningful for most common people. For every gentleman who read scholarly pamphlets and delved into Whig theory and ancient history for an explanation of events, there were dozens of ordinary people who read the Bible and looked to their ministers for an interpretation of the millennial meaning of the Revolution. The Puritans' "city upon a hill" now assumed a new republican character, becoming, in Samuel Adams's evocative phrase, "the Christian Sparta."

It is true that many of the distinguished political leaders of the Revolution were not very emotionally religious. At best, they only passively believed in organized Christianity, and at worst they scorned and ridiculed it. Most were deists or lukewarm churchgoers and scornful of religious emotion and enthusiasm. Washington, for example, was a frequent churchgoer, but he scarcely referred to God as anything but "the Great Disposer of events," and in all his voluminous papers he never mentioned Jesus Christ. Yet this was not true of the great majority of common people. Most ordinary Americans were very religious, and they still conceived of the world in religious terms. As they gained in authority in the course of the Revolution, they brought their religiosity with them.

From the outset of the Revolutionary controversy Americans argued that the dark forces of civic tyranny and religious tyranny were linked. All the new Revolutionary constitutions of 1776 in some way affirmed religious freedom. Yet the constitutional declarations, like that of the Virginia Bill of Rights, that "all men are equally entitled to the free exercise of religion, according to the dictates of conscience" did not necessarily mean that the government would abandon its traditional role in religious matters. To be sure, the official establishment of the Church of England that existed in several of the colonies was immediately eliminated. But the Maryland, South Carolina, and Georgia Revolutionary constitutions authorized their state legislatures to create in place of the Anglican Church a kind of multiple establishment of a variety of religious groups, using tax money to support "the Christian religion."

Virginians especially were divided over the meaning of their 1776 declaration of religious liberty. Liberals like Jefferson and Madison joined growing numbers of Presbyterian and Baptist dissenters to oppose the Anglican clergymen and landowners in a fierce but eventually successful struggle for the complete disestablishment of the Church of England. In 1786 this Virginia struggle climaxed with the passage of Jefferson's memorable Act for Establishing Religious Freedom, with its extraordinary assertion "that our civil rights have no dependence on our religious opinions, any more than on our opinions in physics or geometry." This statement went much further than most ordinary Americans were willing to go. Many of the states retained some vague or general religious qualifications for public office, and both Connecticut and Massachusetts continued to recognize the modified but still official status of the established Congregational church. But the days of such traditional elite-dominated orthodox establishments were numbered.

In the years following the Revolution all the old eighteenth-century monarchical and aristocratic hierarchies, enfeebled and brittle to begin with, fell apart. In thousands of different ways connections that had held people together for centuries were strained and severed, and people were set loose in unprecedented numbers. The Revolution shattered traditional structures of authority, and common people increasingly discovered that they no longer had to accept the old distinctions that had separated them from the upper ranks of the gentry. Ordinary farmers, tradesmen, and artisans began to think they were as good as any gentleman and that they actually counted for something in the movement of events. Not only were the people being equated with God, but half-literate plowmen were being told (even by aristocrats like Thomas Jefferson) that they had as much common or moral sense as learned professors.

As ordinary people became more conscious of their semi-enlightenment, they thought that they had suddenly become wise. Through newspapers, almanacs, tracts, chapbooks, periodicals, lectures, and other media, common people acquired smatterings of knowledge about things that previously had been the preserve of educated elites. And at the same time, they were told that their newly acquired knowledge was as good as that possessed by those who were "college learnt." Under such egalitarian circumstances, truth itself became democratized, and the borders the eighteenth-century Enlightenment had painstakingly worked out between religion and magic, science and superstition, naturalism and supernaturalism, were blurred. Animal magnetism seemed as legitimate as gravity. Dowsing for hidden metals appeared as rational as the workings of electricity. Popular speculations about the lost tribes of Israel seemed as plausible as scholarly studies of the origins of the Indian mounds of the Northwest. And crude folk remedies were even thought to be as scientific as the bleeding cures of enlightened medicine.

The Enlightenment's stress on modern civility and commonsense morality came together with the traditional message of Christian charity to make the decades following the Revolution a great era of benevolence and communalism. Figures as diverse as Jefferson, Samuel Hopkins, and Thomas Campbell told people that all they had to do in the world was to believe in one God and to love other people as themselves. But many of the enlightened leaders and liberal deists scarcely understood what was happening. While Jefferson, for example, continued as late as 1822 to predict that everyone in America would soon become a Unitarian, popular evangelical Christianity was sweeping the country.

The older state churches that had dominated colonial society for a century and a half—the Anglican, Congregational, and Presbyterian—were suddenly supplanted by new and in some cases unheard of religious denominations and sects. As late as 1760 the two great European-like establishments—the Church of England in the South and the Puritan churches in New England—had accounted for more than 40 percent of all congregations in America. By 1790, however, that proportion of religious orthodoxy had dropped below 25 percent. Throughout the country traditional religions were on the defensive.

Everywhere countless numbers of common people were creating new egalitarian and emotionally satisfying evangelical religious communities. While nearly all of the major colonial churches either declined or failed to gain relative to other groups in the years between 1760 and 1790, Methodist and Baptist congregations grew by leaps and bounds. The Baptists expanded from 94 congregations in 1760 to 858 in 1790 to become the single largest religious denomination in America.

The Methodists had no adherents at all in 1760, but by 1790 they had created over 700 congregations to rival in numbers the older Congregational and Presbyterian churches. It would not be long before the Methodists, organized nationally into circuits and locally into classes and served by uneducated itinerant preachers, became the largest church in America.

By 1790 enthusiastic groups of revivalist Baptists, New Light Presbyterians, and Methodists had moved from the margins to the center of American society. But even more remarkable than the growth of these Old World religions was the sudden emergence of new sects and utopian religious groups that no one had ever heard of before—Universal Friends, Universalists, Shakers, and a variety of other splinter groups and millennial sects. Almost overnight the entire religious culture was transformed and the foundations laid for the development of an evangelical religious world of competing denominations that was unique to Christendom.

By destroying traditional structures of authority, the Revolution opened new religious opportunities for the illiterate, the lowly, and the dependent. Both the Baptists and the Methodists encouraged public preaching by women, and even the more conservative Protestant churches began emphasizing a new and special role for women in the process of redemption. Religion was in fact a major public arena in which women could play a substantial role. By the time of the Revolution nearly 70 percent of church members of the New England churches were women, and in the decades following the Revolution this feminization of American Christianity only increased. Some of the most radical sects, like Mother Ann Lee's Shakers and Jemima Wilkinson's Universal Friends, even allowed for female leadership; the Shakers, in fact, became the first American religious group to recognize formally the equality of the sexes at all levels of authority.

The democratic and egalitarian revolution of these years

made it possible for the most common and humble of people to express their emotions and values in ways they could not have earlier. Genteel learning, formal catechisms, even literacy no longer mattered as much as they had in the past, and the new religious groups were able to recruit members from among hitherto unchurched people in the society. Under the influence of the new popular revivalist sects, thousands of African-American slaves became Christianized, and blacks, even black slaves, occasionally emerged as preachers and exhorters. In the 1780s and 1790s a black preacher, Andrew Bryan, organized several Baptist churches in Georgia, including the first Baptist church that whites or blacks in Savannah had ever seen. Both the Baptists and the Methodists at first condemned slavery and welcomed blacks to full membership in their communion. In fact, in parts of the South the first Methodist adherents were black slaves. By 1800 nearly one out of three American Methodists was an African American.

Although we know very little of the actual religious practices in the black churches, white observers emphasized praying, preaching, and especially singing as the central elements of black worship. The black churches in the North and the slave communities in the South stressed the expression of feelings, mixed African traditions with Christian forms, hymns, and symbols, and created religions that fit their needs on their own terms.

But it was not just African Americans who brought more emotion to religion. The Revolution released torrents of popular religiosity and passion into American life, and everywhere ordinary white folk as well as black openly revealed their religious feelings as never before. Visions, dreams, prophesyings, and new emotion-soaked religious seekings acquired a new popular significance, and common people felt freer to express their hitherto repressed popular and superstitious notions. Divining rods, fortune-telling, astrology, treasure-seeking, and folk medicine thrived publicly as they had not since the seventeenth century. Long-existing subterranean folk beliefs and fetishes emerged into the open and blended with traditional Christian practices and the literary culture of the gentry to create a new popular religious amalgam.

In the confusion of post-Revolutionary America, many ordinary people came together anywhere they could—in fields, barns, taverns, or homes—to lay hands on one another, to bathe each other's feet, to offer each other kisses of charity, to form new bonds of fellowship, to lay bare their feelings both physically and vocally, and to Christianize a variety of folk rites. From the "love feasts" of the Methodists to the dancing ceremonies of the Shakers, isolated individuals found in the variety of evangelical "bodily exercises" ungenteel and sometimes bizarre but emotionally satisfying ways of relating to God and to one another. When there were no trained clergy to minister to their inchoate yearnings, they recruited leaders from among themselves. New half-educated, enterprising preachers emerged to mingle exhibitions of book-learning with plain talk and appeals to every kind of emotionalism. Their revivalist techniques were effective because such dynamic folklike processes were better able to meet the needs of rootless egalitarian-minded men and women than were the static churchly institutions based on traditional standards of deference and elite monopolies of orthodoxy. These common people wanted a religion they could personally feel and freely express, and the evangelical denominations offered them that, usually with much enthusiastic folk music and hymn-singing.

Nowhere else in Christendom was religion so fragmented. Yet nowhere else was it so vital. American Protestantism was broken into a multiplicity of denominations, none of which claimed a monopoly of orthodoxy, yet out of whose competition emerged a common Christian truth. There was nothing like it in the Western world.

VII

THE FEDERAL CONSTITUTION

The American Revolution, like all revolutions, could not fulfill all the high hopes of its leaders. Within a decade after Independence was declared, many Revolutionary leaders had come to doubt the way America was going. Not only were they aware that the Confederation was too weak to accomplish its tasks, both at home and abroad, but they were also having second thoughts about the immense power that had been given to the popular state legislatures in 1776. In the mid-1780s frustration with piecemeal changes in the Articles of Confederation came together with mounting concern over examples of legislative tyranny and other political and social conditions in the states to produce a powerful momentum for constitutional change. The result was the federal Constitution of 1787.

This new national Constitution, which replaced the Articles of Confederation, not only limited the authority of the states but also created an unprecedented concentration of power at the federal level. Many Americans could only conclude that the new Constitution represented as radical a change as the Revolution itself. At last, in the eyes of some, the inauguration of a new federal government promised the harmony and stability that would allow America to become a great and glorious nation.

THE CRITICAL PERIOD

For some Americans the 1780s had become a critical period, a point at which the Revolution and the entire experiment in republicanism seemed to be in danger. The very success of the Revolution in opening up opportunities for prosperity to new and lower levels of the population helped to create a sense of crisis among certain members of the Revolutionary elite.

Too many ordinary people, some felt, were distorting republican equality, defying legitimate authority, and blurring those natural distinctions that all gentlemen, even republican gentlemen, thought essential for social order. Everywhere, even among the sturdy independent yeomen—Jefferson's "chosen people of God"—private interests, selfishness, and moneymaking seemed to be destroying social affection and public spirit—the very qualities of virtue that were required of republican citizens. The passing of unjust and confusing laws by the state legislatures—"democratic despotism," it was called—suggested that the people were too self-interested to be good republicans. Some therefore feared that America was doomed to share the fate that had befallen the ancient republics, Britain, and other corrupt nations. Americans, concluded Governor William Livingston of New Jersey, in a common elitist reckoning of 1787, "do not exhibit the virtue that is necessary to support a republican government."

The Revolution had radically democratized the new state legislatures by increasing the number of their members and altering their social character. Men of more humble and more rural origins and less educated than those who had sat in the colonial assemblies now became representatives. In New Hampshire, for example, in 1765 the colonial assembly had contained only thirty-four members, almost all well-to-do gentlemen from the coastal region around Portsmouth. By 1786 the state's House of Representatives had increased to eighty-eight members. Most of these were ordinary farmers or men of moderate wealth, and many were from the western areas of the state. In other states the change was less dramatic but no less significant.

The need to bring the state governments closer to more ordinary people was also reflected in the shifts of most of the state capitals from their colonial locations on the eastern coastline to new sites in the interior—from Portsmouth to

Concord in New Hampshire, from New York City to Albany
in New York, from the dual colonial capitals Burlington and
Perth Amboy to Trenton in New Jersey, from Philadelphia to
Lancaster in Pennsylvania, from Williamsburg to Richmond
in Virginia, from New Bern to Raleigh in North Carolina,
from Charleston to Columbia in South Carolina, and from
Savannah to Augusta in Georgia.

Everywhere electioneering and the open competition for
office increased, along with demands for greater public access
to governmental activities. The number of contested elections and the turnover of legislative seats multiplied. Assembly proceedings were opened to the public, and a growing
number of newspapers (which now included dailies) began to
report legislative debates. Self-appointed leaders, speaking
for newly aroused groups and localities, took advantage of the
enlarged suffrage and the annual elections of the legislatures
(a radical innovation in most states) to seek membership in
the assemblies. New petty entrepreneurs like Abraham Yates,
a part-time lawyer and shoemaker from Albany, and William
Findley, a Scotch-Irish ex-weaver from western Pennsylvania, bypassed the traditional hierarchy and vaulted into political leadership in the states.

Under these circumstances many of the state legislatures
could scarcely fulfill what many Revolutionaries in 1776 had
assumed was their republican responsibility to promote the
general good. In every state, decisions had to be made about
the loyalists and their confiscated property, the distribution of
taxes among the citizens, and the economy. Yet with the general political instability, the common welfare in the various
states was increasingly difficult to define. By the 1780s James
Madison concluded that "a spirit of *locality*" in the state legislatures was destroying "the aggregate interests of the community." This localist spirit, he thought, was a consequence of
having small districts or towns elect members of the state legislatures. Each representative, said Ezra Stiles, president of
Yale College, was concerned only with the special interests of

his electors. Whenever a bill is read in the legislature, "every one instantly thinks how it will affect his constituents."

This kind of narrow-minded politics was not new to America. But the proliferation of economic and social interests in the post-Revolutionary years, along with the greater sensitivity of the enlarged elected popular assemblies to conflicting demands of these interests, now dramatically increased the intensity and importance of such parochial-interest politics. Debtor farmers urged low taxes, the staying of court actions to recover debts, and the printing of paper money. Merchants and creditors called for high taxes on land, the protection of private contracts, and the encouragement of foreign trade. Artisans pleaded for price regulation of agricultural products, the abolition of mercantile monopolies, and tariff protection against imported manufactures. And entrepreneurs everywhere petitioned for legal privileges and corporate grants.

All this political scrambling among contending interests made lawmaking in the states seem chaotic. Laws, as the Vermont Council of Censors said in 1786 in a common complaint, were "altered—realtered—made better—made worse; and kept in such a fluctuating position, that persons in civil commission scarcely know what is law." As James Madison pointed out, more laws were enacted by the states in the decade following independence than in the entire colonial period. Many of them were simply private acts for individuals or resolves redressing minor grievances. But every effort of the legislatures to respond to the excited pleas and pressures of the various interests alienated as many as it satisfied and brought lawmaking itself into contempt.

By the mid-1780s many American leaders had come to believe that the state legislatures, not the governors, were the political authority to be most feared. Not only were some of the legislatures violating the individual rights of property-owners through their excessive printing of paper money and their various acts on behalf of debtors, but in all the states the assemblies also pushed beyond the generous grants of legislative authority of the 1776 Revolutionary constitutions and were absorbing numerous executive and judicial duties—directing military operations, for example, and setting aside court judgments. It began to seem that the once benign legislative power was no more trustworthy than the detested royal power had been. Legislators were supposedly the representatives of the people who annually elected them. But "173 despots would surely be as oppressive as one," wrote Jefferson in 1785 in his *Notes on Virginia.* "An *elective despotism* was not the government we fought for."

These growing fears of tyrannical legislatures forced many leaders to have second thoughts about their popularly elected assemblies. Indeed, the ink was scarcely dry on the Revolutionary state constitutions before some were suggesting that they needed to be revised. Beginning with the New York constitution of 1777 and proceeding through the constitutions of Massachusetts in 1780 and New Hampshire in 1784, constitution-makers now sought a very different distribution of the powers of government from the distribution made in 1776.

Instead of draining all power from the governors and placing it in the legislatures, particularly in the lower houses, as the early state constitutions had done, these later constitutions strengthened the executives, senates, and judiciaries. The Massachusetts constitution of 1780 especially seemed to many to have recaptured some of the best characteristics of the English constitutional balance, which had been forgotten during the popular enthusiasm of 1776. The new Massachusetts governor, with a fixed salary and elected directly by the people, had more of the independence and some of the powers of the old royal governors, including those of appointing to offices and vetoing legislation.

With the Massachusetts constitution as a model, other

constitutional reformers, including Madison and Jefferson in Virginia and James Wilson and Robert Morris in Pennsylvania, worked to revise their own state constitutions. The popular legislatures were reduced in size and their authority curbed. Senates or upper houses were instituted where they did not exist, as in Pennsylvania, Georgia, and Vermont. In states where senates did exist, they were made more stable through longer terms and higher property qualifications for their members. The governors were freed of their dependence on the legislatures and given the central responsibility for government. And judges became independent guardians of the constitutions. By 1790, Pennsylvania, South Carolina, and Georgia had reformed their constitutions along these conservative lines. New Hampshire, Delaware, and Vermont soon followed in the early 1790s.

At the same time that political leaders were attempting to restrengthen the authority of governors, senates, and judges, they also tried to limit the power of the legislatures by appealing to the fundamental law that was presumably embodied in the states' written constitutions. Since many of the constitutions had been created by simple legislative act, it was not easy to distinguish between fundamental and ordinary law.

At first, several of the states had grappled with various devices to distinguish between their fundamental constitutions and ordinary legislation. Some simply declared their constitutions to be fundamental; others required a special majority or successive acts of the legislature for amending the constitution. But none of these measures proved effective against repeated legislative encroachments.

In attempting to solve this problem Americans gradually came to believe that if a constitution was to be truly immune from legislative tampering, it would have to be created, as Jefferson said in 1785, "by a power superior to that of the ordinary legislature." For a solution, Americans fell back on the institution of the convention. In 1775–76 the convention had been merely an ad hoc legislative meeting, lacking legal sanction but made necessary by the crown's refusal to call together the regular representatives of the people. Now, however, the convention became a special alternative institution representing the people and having the exclusive authority to write or amend a constitution. When Massachusetts and New Hampshire came to write new constitutions in the late 1770s and early 1780s, the proper pattern of constitution-making and constitution-altering had become clear. Constitutions were formed by specially elected conventions and then placed before the people for ratification.

With this idea of a constitution as fundamental law immune from legislative encroachment firmly in hand, some state judges during the 1780s began cautiously moving in isolated cases to impose restraints on what the assemblies were enacting as law. In effect, they said to the legislatures, as George Wythe, judge of the Virginia Supreme Court, did in 1782, "Here is the limit of your authority; and, hither, shall you go, but no further." These were the hesitant beginnings of what eventually would come to be called judicial review. Many leaders, however, were as yet unwilling to allow appointed judges to set aside laws that had been made by the people represented in democratically elected legislatures. "This," said a perplexed James Madison in 1788, "makes the Judiciary Department paramount in fact to the Legislature, which was never intended and can never be proper."

As vigorously as all these constitutional reforms of the states were urged and adopted in the 1780s, however, they never seemed sufficient. By the mid-1780s many reformers were thinking of shifting the arena of constitutional change from the states to the nation and were looking to a modification of the structure of the central government as the best and perhaps only answer to America's political and social problems.

Even before the Articles of Confederation were ratified in 1781, the experiences of the war had exposed the weakness of the Congress and had encouraged some Americans to think about making changes in the central government. By 1780 the war was dragging on longer than anyone had expected and the skyrocketing inflation of the paper money used to finance it was unsettling commerce and business. With congressional delegates barred from serving more than three years in any six-year period, leadership in the Confederation was fluctuating and confused. The states ignored congressional resolutions and refused to supply their allotted contributions to the central government. With no ability to raise money, the Congress simply ceased paying interest on the public debt. The Continental Army smoldered with resentment at the lack of pay and began falling apart through desertions and even outbreaks of mutiny. All these circumstances forced mercantile and creditor interests, especially those centered in the mid-Atlantic states, to seek to add to the powers of the Congress. Reformers tried to strengthen the Congress by broadly interpreting the Articles, by directly amending them (which required the consent of all the states), and even by threatening the states with military force.

A shift in congressional leadership in the early eighties allowed these concerned national groups to exert greater influence. Older popular radicals like Richard Henry Lee and Arthur Lee of Virginia and Samuel Adams of Massachusetts were replaced by such younger men as James Madison of Virginia and Alexander Hamilton of New York, who were more interested in authority and stability than in popular democracy. Disillusioned by the ineffectiveness of the Confederation, these nationalists in the Congress set about reversing the localist and power-weakening emphasis of the Revolution. They strengthened the regular army at the expense of the militia and promised pensions to the Continental Army officers. They reorganized the departments of war, foreign affairs, and finance in the Congress and replaced the committees that had been running them with individuals. The key individual in the nationalists' program was Robert Morris, a wealthy Philadelphia merchant who was made superintendent of finance and virtual head of the Confederation in 1781. In order to attach financial and commercial groups to the central government, Morris undertook to stabilize the economy and fund the national debt. He persuaded Congress to recommend to the states that paper-money laws be repealed and to require that the states' contributions to the general expenses be paid in gold or silver. And he sought to establish a national bank and to make federal bonds more secure for investors.

Carrying out this nationalist program depended upon amending the Articles so as to grant the Confederation the power to levy a 5 percent duty on imports. Once the Congress had adequate revenues independent of the states, the Confederation could pay its debts and would become more attractive to prospective buyers of its bonds. Although Morris was able to induce Congress to charter the Bank of North America, the rest of the nationalists' economic proposals narrowly failed. Not only did the states ultimately refuse to approve the impost amendment, but many were slow in supplying the money that had been requisitioned by Congress. Nor was Congress able to get even a restricted authority to regulate commerce.

After the allied victory at Yorktown in October 1781 and the opening of peace negotiations with Great Britain, interest in the Congress declined and some individuals became desperate. The prospect of Congress's demobilizing the army without fulfilling its promises of back pay and pensions created a crisis that brought the United States as close to a military coup d'état as it has ever been. In March 1783, the officers of Washington's army encamped at Newburgh on the Hudson River issued an address to the Congress concerning their pay. They actually plotted some sort of military action against the Confederation. Only when Washington personally intervened and refused to support a movement that was designed, he said, "to open the floodgates of civil discord, and deluge our rising empire in blood" was the crisis averted.

News of the peace in 1783 shattered much of the unionist sentiment that had existed during the war. By December 1783 the Congress, in Jefferson's opinion, had lost much of its usefulness. "The constant session of Congress can not be necessary in time of peace," he said. After clearing up the most urgent business, the delegates should "separate and return to our respective states, leaving only a Committee of the states," and thus "destroy the strange idea of their being a permanent body."

Congressional power, which had been substantial during the war years, now began to disintegrate. The delegates increasingly complained how difficult it was even to gather a quorum. The Congress could not even agree on a permanent home: It wandered from Philadelphia to Princeton to Annapolis to Trenton and finally to New York City. The states reasserted their authority and began taking over the payment of the federal debt that many had earlier hoped to make the cement of union. By 1786 the states had converted nearly one third of the federal securities into state bonds, thus creating a vested interest among public creditors in the sovereignty of the individual states. Under these circumstances the influence of those, as Hamilton called them, "who think continentally" rapidly declined, and the chances of amending the Confederation piecemeal declined with them. The only hope of reform now seemed to lie in some sort of convention of all the states.

In Europe the reputation of the United States dwindled as rapidly as did its credit. The Dutch and French would lend money only at extraordinary rates of interest. Since American ships now lacked the protection of the British flag, many of them were seized by corsairs from the Muslim states of North Africa and their crews were sold into slavery. The

Congress had no money to pay the necessary tribute and ransoms to these Barbary pirates.

Amid a world of hostile monarchical empires the new republican confederacy was even hard-pressed to maintain its territorial integrity. Britain refused to send a minister to the United States and ignored its treaty obligations to evacuate its military posts in the Northwest, claiming that the United States had not honored its own commitments. The treaty of peace had stipulated that the Confederation would recommend to the states that loyalist property confiscated during the Revolution be restored to its owners and that neither side would make laws obstructing the recovery of prewar debts. When the states flouted these treaty obligations, the impotent Confederation could do nothing.

Britain was known to be plotting with the Indians and encouraging separatist movements in the Northwest and in the Vermont borderlands, and Spain was doing the same in the Southwest. Spain in fact refused to recognize American claims to the territory between Florida and the Ohio River. In 1784 in an effort to bring American settlers moving into Kentucky and Tennessee under its control, Spain closed the Mississippi to American trade. Many westerners were ready to deal with any government that could ensure access to the sea for their agricultural produce. As Washington noted in 1784, the western settlers were "on a pivot. The touch of a feather would turn them any way."

In 1785–86, John Jay, a New York aristocrat and the secretary of foreign affairs, negotiated a treaty with the Spanish minister to the United States, Diego de Gardoqui. By the terms of this agreement Spain was opened to American trade in return for America's renunciation of its right to navigate the Mississippi for several decades. Out of fear of being denied an outlet to the sea in the West, the southern states prevented the necessary nine-state majority in the Congress from agreeing to the treaty. But the desire of a majority of seven states to sacrifice western interests for the sake of

northern merchants aroused long-existing sectional jealousies and threatened to shatter the Union.

Despite the efforts of the diplomatic commission of Jefferson, Franklin, and Adams to negotiate liberal commercial
treaties, the mercantilist empires of the major European nations remained generally closed to the new republic in the
1780s. The French were unwilling to take as much American
produce as had been expected, and Britain effectively barred
competitive American goods from its markets while recaptur-
ing American consumer markets for its own goods. The Confederation lacked the authority to retaliate with its own trade
regulations, and several attempts to grant the Congress a
restricted power over commerce were lost amid state and sectional jealousies. The Confederation Congress watched help-
lessly as the separate states attempted to pass ineffectual
navigation acts of their own. By the mid-1780s, for example,
Connecticut was laying heavier duties on goods from Massachusetts than on those from Great Britain.

In the end, the Confederation's inability to regulate commerce finally precipitated reform of the Articles. Jefferson,
Madison, and other leaders with agrarian interests wanted
American farmers free to sell their surplus crops abroad.
They feared that if they were prohibited from doing so the
farmers would sink into lethargy and lose their industrious-
ness. More important, if the United States did not sell its agricultural produce in Europe, it would be unable to pay for
manufactured goods imported from Europe and would therefore be compelled to begin large-scale manufacturing for itself. These developments in turn would eventually destroy the
farmer-citizenry on which republicanism was based and would
create in America the same kind of corrupt, rank-conscious,
and dependent society that existed in Europe. Thus the Confederation desperately needed commercial regulatory power
in order to compel the European states to open their markets
to American agricultural goods.

THE PHILADELPHIA CONVENTION

By 1786 these accumulated pressures made some sort of revision of the Articles inevitable. Virginia's desire for trade regulation led to a convention of several states at Annapolis in September 1786. Those who attended the meeting quickly realized that commerce could not be considered apart from other problems and called for a larger convention in Philadelphia in May of the following year. After several states agreed to send delegates to Philadelphia, the Confederation Congress belatedly recognized the approaching convention and in February 1787 authorized it to revise the Articles of Confederation.

By 1787 almost every political leader in the country, even those who later opposed the new Constitution, expected some new powers to be added to the Confederation Congress. Reform of the Articles in some way or other—particularly by granting the Congress a limited authority to tax and the power to regulate trade—was in the air. This desire to do something about the central government gave the nationalists like James Madison their opportunity, and it helps explain the willingness of people to accede to the meeting at Philadelphia.

Yet few people expected what the Philadelphia Convention eventually created—a new Constitution that utterly transformed the structure of the central government and promised a radical weakening of the states. The extraordinarily powerful national government that emerged from Philadelphia possessed far more than the additional congressional powers that were required to solve the United States' difficulties in credit, commerce, and foreign affairs. Given the Revolutionaries' loyalty to the sovereignty of their states and their deep-rooted fears of centralized governmental authority, the formation of the new Constitution was a truly remarkable achievement. It cannot be explained simply by the obvious weaknesses of the Articles of Confederation.

In the end, it was also the problems within the separate states in the 1780s that made possible constitutional reform of the central government. The unjust and confusing laws coming out of the state legislatures, Madison informed Jefferson in 1787, had become "so frequent and so flagrant as to alarm the most stedfast friends of Republicanism." These popular abuses by the state legislatures, said Madison, "contributed more to that uneasiness which produced the Convention, and prepared the public mind for a general reform, than those which accrued to our national character and interest from the inadequacy of the Confederation to its immediate objects."

In 1786 a rebellion of nearly 2,000 distressed debtor farmers threatened with foreclosure of their mortgages broke out in western Massachusetts. The rebellion, led by a former militia captain, Daniel Shays, closed the courts and threatened to take over a federal arsenal. But more alarming, it occurred in the very state, Massachusetts, that was considered to have the best-balanced constitution. Although Shays's rebels were defeated by militia troops, his sympathizers were victorious at the polls early in 1787. Consequently the newly chosen state representatives soon enacted the kinds of debtor relief legislation that Shays had wanted and that other states were enacting. This legislation convinced many that calling for people to obey the law was a remedy for insurrections only; it did not solve the peculiar problem of legislative tyranny. By voting the sympathizers of Shays into legislative office, the people had made it possible, as one Boston newspaper complained in May 1787, for "sedition itself [to] make laws."

Thus by 1786–87 the reconstruction of the central government was being sought as a means of correcting not only the weaknesses of the Articles but also the democratic despotism and the internal political abuses of the states. A new central government, some believed, could save both the Congress from the states and the states from themselves. New groups joined those already working to invigorate the national government. Urban artisans hoped that a stronger national government would prevent competition from British imports. Southerners, particularly in Virginia, wanted to gain proportional representation of their growing population. And most important, members of the gentry up and down the continent momentarily submerged their sectional and economic differences in the face of what seemed to them a threat to individual liberty from the tyranny of legislative majorities within the states. Creating a new central government was no longer simply a matter of cementing the union, or of standing strong in foreign affairs, or of satisfying the demands of particular creditor, mercantile, and army interests. It was now a matter, as Madison declared, that would "decide forever the fate of republican government."

Fifty-five delegates representing twelve states attended the Philadelphia Convention in the summer of 1787. (Rhode Island, which was acutely jealous of its local autonomy, refused to have anything to do with efforts to revise the Articles.) Although many of the delegates were young men— their average age was forty-two—most were well-educated and experienced members of America's political elite. Thirty-nine had served in Congress at one time or another, eight had worked in the state constitutional conventions, seven had been state governors, and thirty-four were lawyers. One third were veterans of the Continental Army, that great dissolvent of state loyalties, as Washington once called it. Nearly all were gentlemen, "natural aristocrats," who took their political superiority for granted as an inevitable consequence of their social and economic position.

Washington's presence was crucial, but he hesitated to attend. In December 1783 he had voluntarily surrendered his sword to the Congress and had retired to Mount Vernon, promising never again to engage in public affairs. This almost unprecedented willingness to give up political power had electrified the world and had established his worldwide fame as a modern version of the ancient Roman farmer-soldier Cincinnatus. Washington's earlier pledge to withdraw from public life, however, made him reluctant to risk his reputation by getting involved in politics. But friends convinced him that people might think that by not attending the Convention he wanted the federal government to fail so that he could manage a military takeover. So he came and was immediately made president of the Convention.

Some of the other luminaries of the Revolution were not present: Samuel Adams was ill; Thomas Jefferson and John Adams were serving as ministers abroad; and Richard Henry Lee and Patrick Henry, although selected by the Virginia legislature, refused to attend the Convention, Henry saying that he "smelt a rat." The most influential delegations were those of Pennsylvania and Virginia, which included Gouverneur Morris and James Wilson of Pennsylvania and Edmund Randolph, George Mason, and James Madison of Virginia.

The Virginia delegation took the lead and presented the Convention with its first working proposal. This, the Virginia Plan, was largely the effort of the thirty-six-year-old Madison. Short, shy, and soft-spoken, habitually dressed in black, trained to no profession but widely read and possessing an acute and questioning mind, Madison devoted his life to public service. He understood clearly the historical significance of the meeting of the Convention, and it is because of his decision to make a detailed private record of the debates of the Convention that so much is known of what was said that summer in Philadelphia.

Madison's initial proposals for reform were truly radical. They were not, as he pointed out, mere expedients or simple revisions of the Articles; they promised "systematic change" of government. Madison wanted to create a general government that would no longer be a confederation of independent republics but a national republic in its own right. It would operate directly on individuals and be organized as most of the state governments had been organized, with an executive, a bicameral legislature, and a separate judiciary. This national republic would be superimposed on the states. The states would now stand to the central government, in John Jay's words, "in the same light in which counties stand to the state, of which they are parts, viz., merely as districts to facilitate the purposes of domestic order and good government." Thus the radical Virginia Plan provided for a two-house national legislature with the authority to legislate "in all cases to which the states are incompetent" and to veto or "to negative all laws passed by the several states, contravening in the opinion of the National Legislature, the articles of Union." If the national government had the power to veto all state laws, Madison believed, it could then play the same role the English crown had been supposed to play in the British Empire—that of a "disinterested & dispassionate umpire" over clashing interests.

For many in the Philadelphia Convention, however, this Virginia plan was much too extreme. Most delegates were prepared to grant substantial power to the federal government, including the right to tax, regulate commerce, and execute federal laws. But many refused to allow such a weakening of state authority as the Virginia Plan proposed. Opponents of the nationalists, led by delegates from New Jersey, Connecticut, New York, and Delaware, countered with their own proposal, the New Jersey Plan (so-called because it was introduced by William Paterson of New Jersey). This New Jersey Plan essentially amended the Articles of Confederation by adding to the powers of Congress, but at the same time it maintained the basic sovereignty of the states. With two such opposite proposals before it, the Convention approached a crisis in the middle of June 1787.

During the debate that followed, the nationalists, led by Madison and Wilson, were able to retain the basic features of the Virginia Plan and convince a majority of the states at the Convention to reject the New Jersey Plan. Yet the nationalists had to make some concessions. Instead of granting the national legislature a blanket authority "to legislate in all cases to which the separate States are incompetent," as the Virginia Plan proposed, the Convention granted the Congress (in Article I, Section 8 of the Constitution) a list of enumerated powers, including the powers to tax, to borrow and coin money, and to regulate commerce. And instead of giving the national legislature the right to veto harmful state laws, the Convention forbade the states from exercising certain sovereign powers whose abuse had helped to create the crisis of the 1780s. In Article I, Section 10 of the final Constitution, the states were barred from carrying on foreign relations, levying tariffs, coining money, emitting bills of credit, passing ex post facto laws, or doing anything to relieve debtors of the obligations of their contracts. In contrast to the extensive fiscal powers given to the Congress, the states were rendered nearly economically incompetent. Not only did the new Constitution prohibit the states from imposing customs duties—the eighteenth century's most common and efficient form of taxation—but it also denied the states the authority to issue paper money, and thus succeeded in doing what the British government's various currency acts in 1751 and 1764 had tried and generally failed to do.

The Convention decided on a strong and single executive. The president was to stand alone, unencumbered by an executive council except one of his own choosing. With command over the armed forces, with the authority to direct diplomatic relations, with power over appointments to the executive and judicial branches that few state governors possessed, and with a four-year term of office and perpetually reeligible for reelection, the president was a magistrate who, as Patrick Henry later charged, could "easily become king." To ensure the president's independence, he was not to be elected by the legislature, as the Virginia Plan had proposed. Since the Framers believed that few presidential candidates in the future would enjoy wide popular recognition throughout the country, they provided for local elections of "electors" equal in number to the representatives and senators from each state. These electors would cast ballots for the president. But if no candidate received a majority—which in the absence of political parties and organized electioneering was normally expected—the final selection from the five candidates with the most votes would be made by the House of Representatives, with each state delegation having one vote.

The Virginia Plan's suggestion of a separate national judiciary to hold office "during good behavior" was accepted without dispute. The structure of the national judiciary was left to the Congress to devise. The right of this judiciary, however, to set aside acts of the Congress or of the state legislatures was by no means clearly established.

The nationalists in the Convention reluctantly gave way on several crucial issues, particularly on the national legislature's authority to veto state legislation. But they fought longest and hardest to hold on to the principle of proportional representation in both houses of the legislature, and this dispute almost stalemated the Convention. It was decided that both taxation and representation in the House of Representatives ought to be based on population, and not on the states as such or on landed wealth. The nationalists like Madison and Wilson, however, wanted representation in the Senate also to rest on population. Any suggestion that the individual sovereignty of the states ought to be represented equally smacked too much of the old Articles of Confederation. Hence the nationalists came to regard the eventual "Connecticut Compromise," by which each state secured two senators in the upper house of the legislature, as a disastrous defeat.

Although Madison and Wilson lost the battles over the congressional veto of state laws and proportional representation in both houses, they and the other Federalists (as those who supported the Constitution shrewdly came to call themselves) had essentially won the war over the basic nature of the central government. Once the New Jersey Plan, which preserved the essentials of the Articles of Confederation, was rejected on June 19 in favor of the Virginia Plan, the opponents, or Anti-Federalists, found themselves forced, as Richard Henry Lee complained, to accept "this or nothing." And most Anti-Federalists wanted some sort of central government.

Although the Articles of Confederation required that amendments be made by the unanimous consent of the state legislatures, the delegates to the Philadelphia Convention decided to bypass the state legislatures and submit the Constitution to specially elected state conventions for ratification. Approval by only nine of the thirteen states was necessary for the new government to take effect. This transgression of earlier political principles was only one of many to which the Anti-Federalists objected.

THE FEDERALIST–ANTI-FEDERALIST DEBATE

The federal government established by the Philadelphia Convention seemed to violate the principles of 1776 that had guided the Revolutionary constitution-makers. The new Constitution provided for a strong government with an extraordinary amount of power given to the president and the Senate. It also created a single republican state that would span the continent and encompass all the diverse and scattered interests of the whole of American society—an impossibility for a republic according to the best political science of the day. During the debates over ratification in the fall and winter of 1787–88, the Anti-Federalists focused on these Federalist violations of the earlier Revolutionary assumptions about the nature of power and the need for a small homogeneous society in a republican state. They charged that the new federal government resembled a monarchy in its concentration of power at the expense of liberty. Because the society it was to govern was so extensive and heterogeneous, the Anti-

Federalists asserted, the federal government would have to act tyrannically. Inevitably, America would become a single consolidated state, with the individuality of the separate states sacrificed to a powerful national federal government. And this would happen, the Anti-Federalists argued, because of the logic of sovereignty. That powerful principle of eighteenth-century political science, which the British had used so effectively against the colonists in the imperial debate, held that no society could long possess two legislatures: it must inevitably have one final, indivisible lawmaking authority. "We shall find it impossible to please two masters," declared the Anti-Federalists. There could be no compromise: "It is either a federal or a consolidated government, there being no medium as to kind." Because the Constitution was to be the "supreme law of the land," the Anti-Federalists had no doubt that the proposed central government "must eventually annihilate the independent sovereignties of the several states." The doctrine of sovereignty dictated that result.

Despite these formidable Anti-Federalist arguments, the Federalists did not believe that the Constitution repudiated the Revolution and the principles of 1776. They answered the Anti-Federalists not by denying the principle of sovereignty but by relocating it in the people at large. In doing so they forged an entirely new way of thinking about the relation of government to society. It marked one of the most creative moments in the history of political thought.

During the decade since Independence, American political culture had been transformed. Americans, it now appeared clear, had effectively transferred this sovereignty, this final lawmaking authority, from the institutions of government to the people at large. Ever since 1776 the American people, unlike the English, had refused to accept the fact that the election of their representatives eclipsed their existence; in the Americans' view the people "out of doors" continued to act outside of all the official institutions of government.

During the 1780s the people had organized various committees, conventions, and other extralegal bodies in order to voice grievances or to achieve political goals. By doing so, they had continued common practices that had been used during the Revolution itself. Vigilante and mob actions of various kinds had done quickly and efficiently what the new state governments were often unable to do—control prices, prevent profiteering, and punish Tories. Everywhere people had extended the logic of "actual" representation and had sought to instruct and control the institutions of government. Unlike the British in relation to their House of Commons, the American people never surrendered to any political institution or even to all political institutions together their full and final sovereign power.

By 1787–88 all this activity by the people outside of government tended to give reality, even legal reality, to this idea that sovereignty in America resided and remained in the people at large, and not in any specific institutions of government. Only by believing that sovereignty was held by the people outside of government could Americans make theoretical sense of their recent remarkable political inventions—their conception of a written constitution that was immune from legislative tampering, their special constitution-making conventions, their processes of constitutional ratification, and their unusual ideas of "actual" representation. This idea of sovereignty remaining in the people at large rather than being deposited in any institution of government opened up entirely new ways of thinking about government.

To meet the Anti-Federalist arguments against the Constitution, the Federalists were now determined to exploit this new understanding of the ultimate power of the people at large. True, they said, the Philadelphia Convention had gone beyond its instructions to amend the Articles of Confederation. It had drawn up an entirely new government, and it had provided for the new Constitution's ratification by special state conventions. Had not Americans learned during the previous decade that legislatures were not competent to create or to change constitutions? If the federal Constitution was to be truly a fundamental law, then, the Federalists argued, it had to be ratified "by the supreme authority of the people themselves." Hence it was "We the people of the United States," and not the states, that ordained and established the Constitution.

By locating sovereignty in the people rather than in any particular governmental institution, the Federalists could now conceive of what previously had been a contradiction in politics—two legislatures operating simultaneously over the same community—the very issue over which the British Empire had broken. Thus they could answer the principal Anti-Federalist objection to the Constitution—that the logic of sovereignty would dictate that the national Congress would become the one final supreme indivisible lawmaking authority. Only by making the people themselves, and not their representatives in the state legislatures or in the Congress, the final supreme lawmaking authority could the Federalists explain the emerging idea of federalism, that unusual division of legislative responsibilities between the national and state governments in which neither is final and supreme. This idea became the model for similar divisions of legislative power elsewhere in the world.

By asserting that all sovereignty rested with the people, the Federalists were not saying, as theorists had for ages, that all governmental power was merely derived from the people. Instead, they were saying that sovereignty remained always with the people and that government was only a temporary and limited agency of the people—out to the various government officials, so to speak, on a short-term, always recallable loan. No longer could any parts of the state and federal governments, even the popular houses of representatives, ever fully represent the people; instead, all elected parts of the governments—senators and governors and presidents—were now regarded in one way or another as simply partial representatives of the people. This new thinking made nonsense of the age-old theory of mixed or balanced government in which monarchy, aristocracy, and democracy were set against one another. Even though the American governments, at both the state and federal level, contained monarchlike executives and aristocratic senates, they now began to be called unmixed democracies or representative democracies. Since the process of election had become the sole criterion of representation, all elected governmental officials, including senators and executives, were considered equal agents of the people. If judges themselves were likewise considered agents of the people, which is the way many Federalists now described them, then by rights they ought to be elected by the people—which, of course, is precisely what many of the states began to do. Today a majority of states have popularly elected judiciaries.

This new understanding of the relation of the society to government now enabled the Federalists to explain the expansion of a single republican state over a large continent of diverse groups and interests. The Federalists—especially Madison—seized on Scottish philosopher David Hume's radical suggestion that a republican government might operate better in a large territory than in a small one, and ingeniously turned on its head the older assumption that a republic must be small and homogeneous in its interests. The Federalists argued that American experience since 1776 had demonstrated that no republic could be made small enough to avoid the clashing of rival parties and interests. (Tiny Rhode Island was the most faction-ridden of all.) The extended territory of the new national republic was actually its greatest source of strength, wrote Madison in *The Federalist*, No. 10, the most famous of the eighty-five essays that he, Alexander Hamilton, and John Jay wrote in defense of the Constitution in New York. By extending the political arena over the whole nation, Madison concluded, the number of interests and factions in the society would increase to the point where they would check one another and make it less likely that a factious and tyrannical majority could combine in government to oppress the rights of minorities and individuals.

As an added benefit, Madison predicted that the elevated and expanded sphere of national politics would act as a filter, refining the kind of men who would become national leaders. Representatives to the national Congress would have to be elected from relatively large districts—a fact that Madison hoped would inhibit demagogic electioneering. If the people of a particular state—New York, for example—had to elect only ten men to the federal Congress in contrast to the sixty-six they elected to their state legislature, they would be far more likely to ignore the illiberal, narrow-minded men with "factious tempers" and "local prejudices" who had dominated the state legislatures in the 1780s—the Yateses and the Findleys—and instead elect to the new federal government only those educated gentlemen with "the most attractive merit and the most ... established characters." In this way the new federal government would avoid the problems that had plagued the states in the 1780s.

Although the Federalists in creating the Constitution may have intended to curb the populist forces the Revolution had released, the language and principles they used to defend the Constitution were decidedly popular. Indeed, most Federalists felt they had little choice in using democratic rhetoric. The proponents of the Constitution did not need John Dickinson to warn them in Philadelphia that "when this plan goes forth, it will be attacked by the popular leaders. Aristocracy will be the watchword; the Shibboleth among its adversaries." Precisely because the Anti-Federalists, as Hamilton observed in the New York ratifying convention, did talk "so often of an aristocracy," the Federalists were continually compelled in the ratifying debates to minimize, even disguise, the elitist elements of the Constitution. And in fact the Federalists of 1787–88 were not rejecting democratic electoral politics; nor were they trying to reverse the direction of the republican Revolution. They saw themselves rather as saving the Revolution from its excesses, in Madison's words, creating "a republican remedy for the diseases most incident to republican government." They shared a common American agreement that all American governments had to be "strictly republican" and derived "from the only source of just authority—the People."

The Anti-Federalists provided little match for the arguments and the array of talents that the Federalists gathered in support of the Constitution in the ratifying conventions that were held in the states throughout the fall, winter, and spring of 1787–88. Apart from a few distinguished leaders like George Mason and Richard Henry Lee of Virginia, most Anti-Federalists were ordinary state-centered men with only local interests and loyalties. They tended to lack the influence and education of the Federalists, and often they had neither social nor intellectual confidence. They had difficulty making themselves heard both because their speakers, as one Anti-Federalist in Connecticut complained, "were browbeaten by many of those Cicero'es as they think themselves and others of Superior rank," and because much of the press was closed to them. Out of a hundred or more newspapers printed in the late 1780s, only a dozen supported the Anti-Federalists.

Many of the small states—Delaware, New Jersey, Connecticut, and Georgia—commercially dependent on their neighbors or militarily exposed, ratified immediately. The critical struggles took place in the large states of Massachusetts, Virginia, and New York, and acceptance of the Constitution in these states was achieved only by narrow margins and by the promise of future amendments. (Under the leadership of Madison, the first federal Congress attempted to fulfill this promise and proposed twelve amendments to the Constitution. In 1791 ten of them were ratified by the states, and these became the Bill of Rights.) North Carolina and Rhode Island rejected the Constitution, but after New York's ratification in July 1788 the country was ready to go ahead and organize the new government without them.

Despite the difficulties and the close votes in some states, the country's eventual acceptance of the Constitution was almost inevitable. Since the Confederation Congress had virtually ceased to exist, the alternative was governmental chaos. Yet in the face of the great number of wealthy and influential people who supported the Constitution, what in the end remains extraordinary is not the political weakness and disunity of Anti-Federalism but its strength. That large numbers of Americans could actually reject a plan of government that was backed by George Washington and nearly the whole of the "natural aristocracy" of the country said more about the changing character of American politics and society than did the Constitution's acceptance. It was indeed a portent of the democratic world that was coming.

The Anti-Federalists may have lost the contest over the Constitution, but by 1800 they and their Jeffersonian-Republican successors eventually won the larger struggle over what kind of society and culture America was to have, at least for a good part of the nineteenth century. Not only as president in 1801 did Jefferson reduce the power of the national government, but those who had been Anti-Federalists—narrow-minded middling men with interests to promote—soon came to dominate American politics, especially in the North, to a degree that Federalist gentry had never imagined possible.

In the 1780s the arch–Anti-Federalist William Findley had pointed the way. In a debate in the Pennsylvania assembly over the role of interest in public affairs, Findley set forth a rationale for modern democratic interest-group politics that has scarcely been bettered. Unlike his patrician opponents, who continued to hold out a vision of disinterested leadership, Findley argued that since everyone had interests to promote, self-made middling men like himself, who had no lineage, possessed no great wealth, and had never been to college, had as much right to political office as wealthy gentry who had gone to Harvard or Princeton. This was what American equality meant, he said. Furthermore, since everyone did have interests to promote, it was now quite legitimate for candidates for public office to campaign for election on behalf of the interests of their constituents. This was a radical departure from customary practice, for none of the Founders ever thought it was proper for a political leader to campaign for office. In this debate Findley anticipated all of the popular political developments of the next generation—the increased electioneering and competitive politics; the open promotion of interests in legislation, including the proliferation of chartered banks and other private corporations; the emergence of political parties; the extension of the actual and direct representation in government of particular groups, including ethnic and religious groups; and the eventual weakening, if not the repudiation, of the classical republican ideal that legislators were supposed to be disinterested umpires standing above the play of interests. This was democracy as Americans came to know it.

As the Federalists of the 1790s eventually discovered to their dismay, this democracy was no longer a technical term of political science describing the people's representation in the lower houses of representation. And it was no longer a simple form of government that could be skeptically challenged and contested as it had been since the ancient Greeks. Instead, it became the civic faith of the United States to which all Americans must unquestionably adhere. The emergence of this rambunctious middling democracy was the most significant consequence of the American Revolution.

Bibliographic Note

A reader ought to begin with R. R. Palmer's monumental work *The Age of the Democratic Revolution: A Political History of Europe and America, 1760–1800* (2 vols., 1959, 1964), which places the American Revolution in a comparative Atlantic world perspective. Robert Middlekauff, *The Glorious Cause: The American Revolution, 1763–1789* (1982), is a good single-volume account of the Revolution that stresses the military conflict. There are a number of valuable collections of original essays on various aspects of the Revolution, including Stephen G. Kurtz and James H. Hutson, eds., *Essays on the American Revolution* (1973); Alfred F. Young, ed., *The American Revolution* (1976); Young, ed., *Beyond the American Revolution* (1993); the five volumes from the Library of Congress Symposia on the American Revolution (1972–76); and the many volumes on various aspects of the Revolutionary era edited by Ronald Hoffman et al. for the United States Capitol Historical Society.

Among the many attempts to treat the coming of the Revolution from an imperial viewpoint, Lawrence H. Gipson, *The British Empire Before the American Revolution* (15 vols., 1936–70), is the most detailed. Gipson has summarized his massive work in *The Coming of the Revolution, 1763–1775* (1954). For a critical account of British policy, see Robert W. Tucker and David C. Hendrickson, *The Fall of the First British Empire* (1982). Jack P. Greene, *The Quest for Power: The Lower Houses of Assembly in the Southern Royal Colonies, 1689–1776* (1963), stresses the desire of the colonial legislatures for control of their societies. An ingenious but sound study that combines the views of a British and an American historian on the causes of the Revolution is Ian R. Christie and Benjamin W. Labaree, *Empire or Independence, 1760–1776* (1976). Theodore Draper, *A Struggle for Power: The American Revolution* (1996), plays down the importance of ideas in bringing on the Revolution.

Gordon S. Wood, *The Radicalism of the American Revolution* (1992), attempts to show that eighteenth-century monarchical society and culture were transformed by the Revolution. Jon Butler, *Becoming America: The Revolution Before 1776* (2000), argues that the fundamental changes in American society occurred before the Declaration of Independence. On the "consumer revolution," see T. H. Breen, " 'Baubles of Britain': The American and Consumer Revolutions of the Eighteenth Century," in Cary Carson et al., eds., *Of Consuming Interests: The Style of Life in the Eighteenth Century* (1994). Rhys Isaac, *The Transformation of Virginia, 1740–1790* (1982), uses anthropological techniques to illuminate the popular challenges to the Virginia aristocracy. Carl Bridenbaugh, *Cities in Revolt* (1955), attributes the Revolutionary impulse to the cities. Gary B. Nash, *The Urban Crucible: Social Change, Political Consciousness and the Origins of the American Revolution* (1979), stresses urban class conflict in bringing on the Revolution. Stimulating overviews of the mid-eighteenth-century Atlantic world in motion are Bernard Bailyn, *The Peopling of British North America: An Introduction* (1986), and Bailyn, *Voyagers to the West: A Passage in the Peopling of America on the Eve of the Revolution* (1986). The extent of westward migration is ably recounted in Jack M. Sosin, *Revolutionary Frontier, 1763–1783* (1967). Carl Bridenbaugh, *Mitre and Sceptre* (1962), describes the growth of Anglicanism and the effort to establish an American episcopacy in the decades leading up to the Revolution. J. C. D. Clark, *The Language of Liberty, 1660–1832* (1994), sees the Revolution as a civil war over religion.

The opening years of the reign of George III were the subject of some of the most exciting historical scholarship in the twentieth century—largely the work of Sir Lewis Namier and his students. Namier and his followers exhaustively demonstrated that George III was not seeking to destroy the British constitution, as nineteenth-century historians had argued, and that in 1760 party government with ministerial responsibility to Parliament lay very much in the future. Namier's chief works include *The Structure of Politics at the Accession of George III* (2d ed., 1957) and *England in the Age of the American Revolution* (2d ed., 1961). For detailed studies of British politics in the Revolutionary era, see P. D. G. Thomas's three volumes on the several phases of the imperial crisis. For additional works, see Paul Langford, *The First Rockingham Administration: 1765–1766* (1973); John Brooke, *The Chatham Administration, 1766– 1768* (1956); Bernard Donoughue, *British Politics and the American Revolution: The Path to War, 1773–1775* (1964); and Eligia H. Gould, *The Persistence of Empire: British Political Culture in the Age of the American Revolution.* A good biography of George III is John Brooke, *King George III* (1972). For a study that reconciles the Whig and Namierite interpretations, see John Brewer, *Party Ideology and Popular Politics at the Accession of George III* (1976).

On the British military in America, see John Shy, *Toward Lexington: The Role of the British Army in the Coming of the American Revolution* (1965), and Ned R. Stout, *The Royal Navy in America, 1760–1776* (1973).

On American resistance, see especially Pauline Maier, *From Resistance to Revolution* (1972), which stresses the limited and controlled character of American opposition. On urban mobs, see Paul A. Gilje, *The Road to Mobocracy: Popular Disorder in New York City, 1763–1834* (1987).

On other irritants and incidents in the imperial relationship, see Joseph A. Ernst, *Money and Politics in America, 1755–1775* (1973); Carl Ubbelohde, *The Vice-Admiralty Courts and the American Revolution* (1960); M. H. Smith, *The Writs of Assistance Case* (1978); Hiller Zobel, *The Boston Massacre* (1970); Benjamin W. Labaree, *The Boston Tea Party* (1964); and David Ammerman, *In the Common Cause: American Response to the Coercive Acts of 1774* (1974).

Among the many local studies of American resistance are Carl Becker, *The History of Political Parties in the Province of New York, 1760–1776* (1909); Edward Countryman, *A People in Revolution: The American Revolution and Political Society in New York, 1760–1790* (1981); David S. Lovejoy, *Rhode Island Politics and the American Revolution, 1760–1776* (1958); Theodore Thayer, *Pennsylvania Politics and the Growth of Democracy, 1740–1776* (1954); Richard Ryerson, *"The*

Revolution Is Now Begun": The Radical Committees of Philadelphia, 1765–1776 (1978); Patricia Bonomi, *A Factious People: Politics and Society in Colonial New York* (1971); Jere R. Daniel, *Experiment in Republicanism: New Hampshire Politics and the American Revolution, 1741–1794* (1970); Richard D. Brown, *Revolutionary Politics in Massachusetts* (1970); and Ronald Hoffman, *A Spirit of Dissension: Economics, Politics, and the Revolution in Maryland* (1973). For studies of some of the leading Revolutionaries and Founders, see John C. Miller, *Sam Adams* (1936); Richard R. Beeman, *Patrick Henry* (1974); Merrill Peterson, *Thomas Jefferson and the New Nation* (1970); Joseph Ellis, *American Sphinx: The Character of Thomas Jefferson* (1997); Ellis, *Founding Brothers: The Revolutionary Generation* (2001); Carl Van Doren, *Benjamin Franklin* (1938); Eric Foner, *Tom Paine and Revolutionary America* (1976); Richard Brookhiser, *Alexander Hamilton: American* (1999); C. Bradley Thompson, *John Adams and the Spirit of Liberty* (1998); David McCullough, *John Adams* (2001); Marcus Cunliffe, *George Washington: Man and Monument* (1958); James Thomas Flexner, *Washington: The Indispensable Man* (1974); and Garry Wills, *Cincinnatus: George Washington and the Enlightenment* (1984).

Modern interest in the ideas of the Revolution dates back to the 1920s and '30s with the studies of constitutional law and natural rights philosophy by Carl Becker, *The Declaration of Independence* (1922), and Charles H. McIlwain, *The American Revolution: A Constitutional Interpretation* (1923), among others. While these books emphasized formal political theory, others explicitly treated the ideas as propaganda. See Philip Davidson, *Propaganda and the American Revolution, 1763–1783* (1941), and Arthur M. Schlesinger, *Prelude to Independence: The Newspaper War on Britain, 1764–1776* (1958).

In the 1950s serious attention was paid to the determinative influence of ideas in Clinton Rossiter, *Seedtime of the Republic* (1953), and especially in Edmund S. Morgan and Helen M. Morgan, *The Stamp Act Crisis* (1953), which focused on the issue of parliamentary sovereignty. Only in the 1960s, however, with Bernard Bailyn's *Ideological Origins of the American Revolution* (1967) did historians perceive the Revolutionary ideas as ideology—that is, as a configuration of ideas giving meaning and force to events—and begin to recover the cultural distinctiveness of the late-eighteenth-century world. Bailyn's book was based in part on the rediscovery of the radical Whig tradition by Caroline Robbins, *The Eighteenth-Century Commonwealth-*

men (1959). J. R. Pole, *Political Representation in England and the Origin of the American Republic* (1966); Trevor H. Colbourn, *The Lamp of Experience: Whig History and the Beginnings of the American Revolution* (1965); and Isaac F. Kramnick, *Bolingbroke and His Circle* (1968), have further contributed to an understanding of the sources of the Revolutionary tradition. For detailed analyses of the Americans' legal positions in the imperial debate see the many books of John Phillip Reid. Jack P. Greene, *Peripheries and Center* (1986) sets the constitutional issues of federalism in perspective.

The loyalist reaction is analyzed in William H. Nelson, *The American Tory* (1961); Robert M. Calhoon, *The Loyalists in Revolutionary America, 1760–1781* (1973); and Bernard Bailyn, *The Ordeal of Thomas Hutchinson* (1974). A vitriolic account by a loyalist of the causes of the Revolution is Peter Oliver, *Origin and Progress of the American Rebellion,* ed. Douglass Adair and John A. Schutz (1961).

On the military actions of the Revolutionary War, the best brief account is Willard M. Wallace, *Appeal to Arms* (1951). Don Higginbotham, *The War of American Independence* (1971), and John Shy, *A People Numerous and Armed: Reflections on the Military Struggle for American Independence* (1976), best appreciate the unconventional and often guerrilla character of the war. The fullest account of British strategy is Piers Mackesy, *The War for America, 1775–1783* (1964). On the British commanders in chief, see Ira Gruber, *The Howe Brothers and the American Revolution* (1972), and William Willcox, *Portrait of a General: Sir Henry Clinton in the War of Independence* (1964). Paul H. Smith, *Loyalists and Redcoats* (1964), describes British attempts to mobilize the loyalists. A particularly imaginative study is Charles Royster, *A Revolutionary People at War: The Continental Army and American Character, 1775–1783* (1979). On the Americans' difficulties in the war, see two important works by Richard Buel, Jr., *Dear Liberty: Connecticut's Mobilization for the Revolutionary War* (1980) and *In Irons: Britain's Naval Supremacy and the American Revolutionary Economy* (1998).

On the diplomacy of the Revolution the older standard account is Samuel Flagg Bemis, *The Diplomacy of the American Revolution* (1935). See also William C. Stinchcombe, *The American Revolution and the French Alliance* (1969), and Jonathan Dull, *A Diplomatic History of the American Revolution* (1985). Richard B. Morris, *The Peacemakers* (1965), is a full study of the peace negotiations. For a discussion of the Model Treaty and the Americans' new attitude toward diplomacy, see Felix Gilbert, *To the Farewell Address* (1961).

For a summary of the history-writing covering the eighteenth-century tradition of republicanism, see Robert E. Shalhope, "Toward a Republican Synthesis: The Emergence of an Understanding of Republicanism in American Historiography," *The William and Mary Quarterly*, 3d ser., 29 (1972). Studies emphasizing the peculiar character of this tradition include J. G. A. Pocock, *The Machiavellian Moment* (1975); Franco Venturi, *Utopia and Reform in the Enlightenment* (1971); Gerald Stourzh, *Alexander Hamilton and the Idea of Republican Government* (1970); and Gordon S. Wood, *The Creation of the American Republic, 1776–1787* (1969). Garry Wills, *Inventing America: Jefferson's Declaration of Independence* (1978), stresses the importance of Scottish moral sense philosophy and the natural sociability of people in Jefferson's thought. But see also Andrew Brustein, *Sentimental Democracy: The Evolution of America's Romantic Self-Image* (1999). Pauline Maier, *American Scripture: Making the Declaration of Independence* (1997), emphasizes the contributions of the Congress and other Americans to the Declaration. On the origins of the Americans' conception of the individual's relationship to the state, see James H. Kettner, *The Development of American Citizenship, 1608–1870* (1978). For the influence of antiquity, see Carl J. Richard, *The Founders and the Classics* (1994).

The fullest account of state constitution-making and politics is Allan Nevins, *The American States During and After the Revolution, 1775–1789* (1924). Among the most significant of the state studies are Philip A. Crowl, *Maryland During and After the Revolution* (1943); Jean B. Lee, *The Price of Nationhood: The American Revolution in Charles County* [Md.] (1994); Richard P. McCormick, *Experiment in Independence: New Jersey in the Critical Period, 1781–1789* (1950); Irwin H. Polishook, *Rhode Island and the Union, 1774–1795* (1969); Robert J. Taylor, *Western Massachusetts in the Revolution* (1954); and Alfred F. Young, *The Democratic Republicans of New York: The Origins, 1763–1797* (1967). Merrill Jensen, in *The Articles of Confederation . . . 1774–1781* (1940) stresses the achievements of the Articles. The best history of the Continental Congress is Jack N. Rakove, *The Beginnings of National Politics* (1979).

The starting point for appreciating the social changes of the Revolution is the short essay by J. Franklin Jameson, *The American*

Revolution Considered as a Social Movement (1926). For modern appraisals, see Ronald Hoffman and Peter J. Albert, eds., *The Transforming Hand of Revolution* (1995). J. Kirby Martin, *Men in Rebellion: Higher Government Leaders and the Coming of the American Revolution* (1973); Jackson T. Main, *The Upper House in Revolutionary America, 1763–1788* (1967); and Main, "Government by the People: The American Revolution and the Democratization of the Legislatures," *The William and Mary Quarterly,* 3d ser., 28 (1966), document the displacement of elites in politics during the Revolution. Chilton Williamson, *American Suffrage from Property to Democracy, 1760–1860* (1960), describes the expansion of voting rights. A neat account of Concord, Massachusetts, in the Revolution is Robert A. Gross, *The Minutemen and Their World* (1976).

A helpful survey of American social history is Rowland Berthoff, *An Unsettled People* (1971). But it has not replaced the encyclopedic History of American Life Series edited by Arthur M. Schlesinger and Dixon Ryan Fox. The volume covering the Revolutionary era is Evarts B. Greene, *The Revolutionary Generation, 1763–1790* (1943). Population developments are summarized by J. Potter, "The Growth of Population in America, 1700–1860," in David Glass and D. E. Eversley, eds., *Population in History* (1965).

For economic developments, see the appropriate chapters in John J. McCusker and Russell R. Menard, *The Economy of British America, 1607–1789* (1985). On the commercial effects of the Revolution, see Curtis P. Nettles, *The Emergence of a National Economy, 1775–1815* (1962); Robert A. East, *Business Enterprise in the American Revolutionary Era* (1938); Thomas M. Doerflinger, *A Vigorous Spirit of Enterprise: Merchants and Economic Development in Revolutionary Philadelphia* (1986); John J. McCusker et al., eds., *The Economy of Early America: The Revolutionary Period, 1763–1790* (1988); and Cathy Matson and Peter S. Onuf, *A Union of Interests* (1989).

On the plight of the loyalists, see Wallace Brown, *The Good Americans* (1969), and Mary Beth Norton, *The British-Americans: The Loyalist Exiles in England, 1774–1789* (1972). On the Indians, see Colin G. Calloway, *The American Revolution in Indian Country* (1995); and Richard White, *The Middle Ground: Indians, Empires, and Republics in the Great Lakes Region, 1650–1815* (1991).

On the Enlightenment, see Henry May, *The Enlightenment in America* (1976), and Robert A. Ferguson, *The American Enlightenment,*

1750–1820 (1994). The standard survey is Russell B. Nye, *The Cultural Life of the New Nation, 1776–1830* (1960). See also Kenneth Silverman, *A Cultural History of the American Revolution* (1976), and Joseph J. Ellis, *After the Revolution: Profiles of Early American Culture* (1979). On Freemasonry, see the superb book by Steven C. Bullock, *Revolutionary Brotherhood... 1730–1840* (1996). A particularly important study of education is Carl F. Kaestle, *The Evolution of an Urban School System* (1973). On the forming of American nationhood, see David Waldstreicher, *In the Midst of Perpetual Fetes... 1776–1820* (1997). Ruth H. Bloch, *Visionary Republic: Millennial Themes in American Thought, 1756–1800* (1985), and Nathan O. Hatch, *The Democratization of Christianity* (1989) illuminate the millennial and popular evangelical movements in the Revolution.

On women, see Mary Beth Norton, *Liberty's Daughters: The Revolutionary Experience of American Women, 1750–1800* (1980); Linda Kerber, *Women of the Republic: Intellect and Ideology in Revolutionary America* (1980); and Rosalie Zagarri, *A Woman's Dilemma: Mercy Otis Warren and the American Revolution* (1995). Benjamin Quarles, *The Negro in the American Revolution* (1961), and Sylvia Frey, *Water from the Rock: Black Resistance in a Revolutionary Age* (1991) are the best studies of the contribution of blacks to the Revolution. On slavery and opposition to it, see Philip Morgan, *Slave Counterpoint: Black Culture in the Eighteenth-Century Chesapeake and Lowcountry* (1998); Ira Berlin, *Many Thousands Gone* (1998); Winthrop Jordan, *White over Black: American Attitudes Toward the Negro, 1550–1812* (1968); and David Brion Davis, *The Problem of Slavery in the Age of Revolution, 1770–1823* (1975). On the abolition of slavery in the North, see Arthur Zilversmit, *The First Emancipation* (1967).

John Fiske, *The Critical Period of American History* (1888), popularized the Federalist view of the Confederation for the nineteenth century. Merrill Jensen, *The New Nation* (1950), minimizes the crisis of the 1780s and explains the movement for the Constitution as the work of a small but dynamic minority. Clarence L. Ver Steeg, *Robert Morris, Revolutionary Financier* (1954), is the major study of that important figure.

Forrest McDonald, *E Pluribus Unum: The Formation of the American Republic, 1776–1790* (1965), describes the commercial scrambling by the Americans in the 1780s. The best account of the army and the Newburgh Conspiracy is Richard H. Kohn, *Eagle and Sword: The Fed-*

eralists and the Creation of the Military Establishment in America, 1783–1802 (1975). Frederick W. Marks III, *Independence on Trial* (1973), analyzes the foreign problems contributing to the making of the Constitution. The best short survey of the Confederation period is still Andrew C. McLaughlin, *The Confederation and the Constitution, 1783–1789* (1905). But see also Richard B. Morris, *The Forging of the Union, 1781–1789* (1987), and Merrill Jensen, *The New Nation* (1950).

Charles Beard's book *An Economic Interpretation of the Constitution* (1913) sought to explain the Constitution as something other than the consequence of high-minded idealism. It became the most influential history book ever written in America. Beard saw the struggle over the Constitution as a "deep-seated conflict between a popular party based on paper money and agrarian interests and a conservative party centered in the towns and resting on financial, mercantile, and personal property interests generally." While Beard's particular proof for his thesis—that the Founders held federal securities that they expected would appreciate in value under a new national government—has been demolished, especially by Forrest McDonald, *We the People* (1958), his general interpretation of the origins of the Constitution still casts a long shadow. Jackson T. Main, *Political Parties Before the Constitution* (1974), finds a "cosmopolitan"-"localist" split within the states over the Constitution. Gordon S. Wood, *The Creation of the American Republic, 1776–1787* (1969), working through the ideas, discovers a similar social, but not strictly speaking a "class," division over the Constitution.

The best history of the Convention is still Max Farrand, *The Framing of the Constitution of the United States* (1913), which sees the Constitution as "a bundle of compromises" designed to meet specific defects of the Articles. For a brief authoritative biography of the "father of the Constitution," see Jack N. Rakove, *James Madison and the Creation of the American Republic* (1991). Rakove's book *Original Meanings* (1996) is crucial for anyone interested in what the Constitution meant to the Founders.

Max Farrand, ed., *The Records of the Federal Convention of 1787* (4 vols., 1911, 1937); and Merrill Jensen et al., eds., *The Documentary History of the Ratification of the Constitution* (1976–) are collections of the important documents. Jacob Cooke, ed., *The Federalist* (1961), is the best edition of these papers. Sympathetic studies of the Anti-Federalists are Jackson T. Main, *The Antifederalists... 1781–1788*

(1961), and Saul Cornell, *The Other Founders: Anti-Federalism and the Dissenting Tradition in America, 1788–1828* (1999). See also Robert A. Rutland, *The Birth of the Bill of Rights, 1776–1791* (1955). The papers of the Founders—Jefferson, Franklin, Hamilton, John Adams, Madison, Washington, and others—are already published or are currently being published in mammoth scholarly editions.

INDEX

GORDON S. WOOD received his B.A. from Tufts University and his Ph.D. from Harvard University. He has taught at the College of William and Mary, Harvard, and the University of Michigan. Since 1969 he has been at Brown University, where he is a professor of history. In 1970 his book *The Creation of the American Republic 1776–1787* was nominated for the National Book Award and received the Bancroft and John H. Dunning prizes. In 1993 he won the Pulitzer Prize for *The Radicalism of the American Revolution*. He lives in Providence, Rhode Island.

A NOTE ON THE TYPE

The principal text of this Modern Library edition was set in a digitized version of Janson, a typeface that dates from about 1690 and was cut by Nicholas Kis, a Hungarian working in Amsterdam. The original matrices have survived and are held by the Stempel foundry in Germany. Hermann Zapf redesigned some of the weights and sizes for Stempel, basing his revisions on the original design.